PRICELESS

PRICELESS

The Autobiography

Rodney Marsh

HEADLINE

First published in 2001
by HEADLINE BOOK PUBLISHING

10 9 8 7 6 5 4 3 2 1

British Library Cataloguing in Publication Data

Marsh, Rodney
        Priceless : my autobiography
        1.Marsh, Rodney
        2.Soccer players – England – Biography
        I.Title
        796.3'34'092

ISBN 0 7553 1000 4

Typeset by
Letterpart Limited, Reigate, Surrey

Printed and bound in Great Britain by
Mackays of Chatham PLC, Chatham, Kent

HEADLINE BOOK PUBLISHING
A division of Hodder Headline
338 Euston Road
LONDON NW1 3BH

www.headline.co.uk
www.hodderheadline.com

contents

acknowledgements

Thank you to: Alex Henderson for insisting on quality and accuracy in co-authoring this book; Melissa Chappell at RAM Sports for her commitment and efforts in collaborating with Alex; Ian Marshall at Headline for his direction and focus and Jon Robinson for his help with additional research.

Lastly, and most importantly, I would like to thank my family, Jean, Joanna and Jonathan, for helping to refresh my perspective and for their support throughout my life, particularly through the difficult times.

CHAPTER 1

schooled with a strap

I was schooled with a strap right across my back
But it's all right now, in fact, it's a gas . . .

Mick Jagger and Keith Richards,
The Rolling Stones, 1969

I love football passionately – always have and always will. From the earliest age I can remember, all I ever wanted to be was a footballer. It's said that only one in 100,000 kids becomes a professional player and only one in a million goes on to play for his country. Fortunately, and against a lot of odds, I managed to achieve both. Coming from the East End of London post Second World War, your prospects weren't too great. Ask anyone who was around the area at that time and they'll tell you the same.

Actually, I was born in Hertfordshire. In 1944 Hitler's doodle-bug flying bombs were threatening to pummel London's docklands once more and my mother, Lilian, was evacuated to Hatfield for the final three days of her pregnancy. She was back home to the rubble with me before anyone had missed her. They were tough old birds in those days.

My dad, Billy, was mad on football so it was great for him to have a son to play with. When Mum and I returned to London, he was still celebrating England's recent 8–0 massacre of Scotland at, of all places, Maine Road.

To say my formative years were a bit tough doesn't even begin to tell the story. If you still had your own teeth by the time you were 10 they called you a sissy. In those days, not many made it out of the East End slums honestly. To get a better life you had to fight your way out of the gutter, literally – route one was to become a boxer. If you couldn't fight, your next best chance was as a pop singer, or maybe the stage, if you had the front, or if you were really lucky, you became a footballer.

I was hopeless in the ring and couldn't sing to save my life, but with a football I knew I could put on a show with the best of them. All I needed was the chance. Even then I was positive I had what it took to make it, but I had an added incentive – Kennedy, my father's big thick brown belt with its menacingly glistening metal buckle. That's what I would get across my backside if I stepped out of line at home, no hesitation. God forbid what would have happened if I'd been in trouble with the law. Kennedy might well have helped keep me out of jail, but at what price? I was so terrified of that brutal instrument of discipline that I never once plucked up the courage to ask my father why he called his belt Kennedy. I am still haunted by it to this day. In fact, my stomach goes cold even thinking about it.

Of course, I could be a bit of a pain in the arse. Sometimes I used to give my mother too much lip, so maybe I needed a bit of correction; but no kid deserved Kennedy's harshness. I can vividly remember one day when I was no more than eight or nine years old and being, as a lot of us are at that age, a little bit cheeky. My dad's response was predictable.

'Do you want Kennedy, son? 'Cos you're going to get some if you keep on.'

I'll never understand why on that occasion I had more bottle than usual. My mouth, not for the last time in my life, got the better of me. Stupidly I replied, 'Thank you. That would be nice. Yeah, I'll have some of that then.'

My dad went ballistic and Kennedy was out in a flash.

Desperately I tried to duck under the kitchen table but I couldn't get my hand off the tabletop quick enough and screamed in agony as metal smashed into bone. There was blood everywhere and I was too petrified of another ferocious attack to go to the hospital to have stitches. My dad was sorry. Cowering under the table, I could see that he was remorseful. He hadn't intended to be that vicious. He just lost it completely. But the damage had been done. I was so terrified that he would beat me again with Kennedy that things between us were never the same. I had to protect myself and not just physically. Experiences like that can be as painful mentally and I suppose that's why I have built up some of the barriers I have. Perhaps being an only child didn't help.

For the best part of my life I couldn't cry. I became completely emotionless. For instance, when my mother died my attitude was that's it then. Mum's dead. Got to move on. I loved her but I couldn't show my feelings. Jean, my wife, says I was always very blasé in situations like that. When I think about it now it makes me feel sick to the stomach but I'm sure that persona was the result of the relationship I had with my dad.

After that moment with Kennedy I was never able to tell my dad that I loved him. Twenty-seven years later, on the day before he passed away, he looked me in the eyes and hugged me. It was one of the most poignant moments in my life, and I couldn't find it in me to hug him back – something I bitterly regret.

My mother had her moments, too. Once I poked my head around the door and started to take the mickey out of her. I suppose I went a bit too far but in temper she picked up a metal brush and threw it at me. The brush struck me right between the eyes and again there was blood everywhere. She didn't mean it and I was bang out of order. Still, I was only a kid.

I often felt safer out of my parents' way and spent most of my spare time with my mates, playing all kinds of sports. Mum and Dad encouraged me a lot. My dad had been an amateur footballer and a boxer, too. I had a bout at Eton Manor in Hackney once as an 11 year old. The right walloping I took easily ensured I never went back.

I played football from the first moment I can remember. In my initial trials for Hackney Schools they asked me what position I'd like to play. I said that I was best at inside-forward, No. 10, so of course they played me at right-back. Obvious, really, isn't it? After you've scored buckets of goals the best spot for you is as a defender. Still, that's the Football Association's coaching system for you, but it wasn't until later that I realised what total prats they are.

At right-back I was useless. I couldn't tackle, wasn't quick and couldn't head a ball. Not surprisingly, I was taken off after 45 minutes, but I wasn't deterred one bit. Even at that age I knew I had the ability to score. In almost every game I played I hit the target. I was that confident. Once I scored 13 in a game for Alexander Boys' Club, my local side. Luckily enough, Hackney Schools gave me another chance because of the number of goals I was banging in for my school. I went to Joseph Priestley, where Sir Alan Sugar would follow a few years later and where 'monster' football agent Eric Hall had previously learned some of the tricks of his trade – whatever they are.

Nonetheless, I couldn't get the centre-forward's shirt because the lad in possession was also the captain. I was stuck out on the left wing. The boy who kept me out was Ron 'Chopper' Harris who, ironically, in the sixties and early seventies became one of the best defenders in the game. I always thought Chopper was a great defender and he went on to skipper Chelsea to their FA Cup and European Cup-Winners' Cup victories.

Hackney Schools went on to win the schools national championships. In the final I scored a hat-trick in the 3–0 win. You should have seen Ron's face. It was a picture. For once, he had to take second billing and was less than pleased with me.

Generally, as a kid I'd come home from school, do my homework and go straight to the local youth club. There, we'd play football, table tennis and cricket, all of which I really enjoyed. A few years later I had to choose between joining Middlesex colts as a cricketer or Fulham. For someone from the East End that was really something. I mean, Lord's is the home of cricket, but it wasn't a tough decision because I loved football.

I never liked my parents to watch me play. I was embarrassed if they were there. It didn't put my dad off, though. He would come wearing a false moustache and beard or a ridiculous hat and scarf so I wouldn't recognise him. It was laughable really. With my mum it was even worse. I played for Alexander Boys' in the final of the All London Club Championships. I'd already scored two goals and as I was going for a third, one of the opposing team's parents yelled, 'Break his fucking legs.' The next second, I was hacked down right in front of my mother. She turned and smashed the guy in the face with an umbrella. They had to pull her off him. That was enough. I was never going to have them there again.

My dad always wanted me to be a footballer and by then my name was getting around as a promising 14 year old. I was determined to make it. I was too scared of Kennedy to waste any opportunity that came my way.

I've had my ups and downs. The highs have been superb and thankfully I've never slopped out at Wandsworth Prison, so I haven't got any moans. In fact, I've had a great life, and have a lovely family with my wife Jean and my children, Joanna and Jonathan.

As a player, the most ecstatic I've been is when I scored the equaliser for Queens Park Rangers against West Bromwich Albion in the 1967 League Cup final. We went on to beat the Baggies 3–2 and were the first Third Division side to win a Wembley final. I get a warm glow when I hear people say that my goal was the best they have ever seen at Wembley.

It's indescribable how you feel when you score in front of a 100,000 Wembley full house. I wish everybody who loves football had the opportunity to do something like that just once in his life. I've tried to explain the feeling on so many occasions and I've never managed to convey the sheer ecstasy of the moment. Everything is heightened; veins in your neck start to pump as blood surges through them. The sounds are deafening and surreal. You can smell every blade of grass; every colour is blinding. There is such an adrenalin rush that you think your head is going to explode. You feel out of control. It's almost an epiphany. I can understand completely the crazy celebrations that you see from players all around the world today. To score a goal in any game is great, but doing it at the highest level leaves an ineffable feeling.

Thanks to football I've rubbed shoulders with some of the most famous people in the world – Pele, Muhammad Ali, Sir Elton John, Sir Paul McCartney, Henry Kissinger, Faye Dunaway, Rod Stewart, Phil Collins, Sir Richard Branson, and the Sheikh of Dubai, among others. It's all a world away from the two-roomed dilapidated flat in Poplar where I first lived with my mum and dad. We didn't even have an inside toilet. Nobody did in those days. If you needed to go in the night, you went to the red-brick outhouse in the back garden with a candle and the Sunday newspaper.

We never had a bath. Once a month we'd all troop down to the local public baths, like everyone else in our street. I remember the first time I went. Up until then I'd washed in the kitchen in an old metal tub that we kept in a shed. One day, after I had heard one of my mates boasting about having a bath, I begged my dad to take me. So off we went to Shoreditch Baths where it cost nine old pence, about the cost of two phone calls today, for the privilege.

Eventually, we moved to a three-storey, three-bedroomed Victorian terraced house in Stoke Newington. The place had been divided into three and 11 members of two other families lived in the other two flats. Unfortunately, we still had just one bedroom and a living room. For the first 10 years of my life I slept on a mattress in the corner of my parents' bedroom. There was no privacy. I didn't have a proper bed of my own until I was 11 and then it was still in the same room as Mum and Dad. Compared with the other kids who lived in the house, I suppose I was lucky.

We were incredibly poor. My dad was a docker all his life, just like his father. My mother was a professional bingo player. Today she'd be called a homemaker. Mum never went out to work in her life, she raised a family, which was quite normal then. Holidays? The best we did was an occasional day trip to Southend. About twice a week we'd eat tripe and onions because it cost next to nothing. On other days we'd have egg and chips. I don't think my parents went out to a restaurant once in their lives. You can't count fish and chips wrapped in newspaper on a Friday night or an occasional visit to Cooke's, the local pie and mash shop, can you?

Every Friday my dad would go on what was known then as a 'jolly up'. He would go round all the local shops and steal something from them – a box of chocolates from one, some fruit from another and so on. Then Dad would come home with a bag full of his proceeds for a big tuck-in.

Both my parents were products of the East End school of hard knocks. When they married, my dad was 27 and my mum was 23. Mum was born in Shoreditch and went to live in Islington. Fortunately, her family was fairly normal. My dad's family was a totally different kettle of fish. Originally from Bow, he later moved to Poplar where he set up home with Mum. It didn't matter where the Marshes or the Dredges went, though – locals knew about them. They were known in the East End for violence. No wonder many of them turned out to be useful amateur boxers. My dad's brother Albert was a terrific amateur fighter. In many other ways he was artistic – and extraordinarily violent. As a schoolboy, he couldn't be beaten in the ring; or out of it, come to that.

My grandmother used to play the piano in one of the local pubs. One night she was playing a few songs in the bar. My granddad was there, and Albert, who never drank – didn't touch a drop in his entire life. Also in the bar was a bunch of Swedish sailors who had just docked. Apparently there were about eight of them and they were giving my grandma some stick, really taking the piss. Albert stood it for about five minutes, then politely escorted his parents from the room to save them from the abuse. The sailors were cheering and yelling but it all went quiet when Albert went back inside. When he rejoined his mum and dad outside, there wasn't a sailor left standing; in front of a horrified publican, he had also had the nerve to phone for an ambulance.

It was tragic what happened to him. When he was in the army he was buried alive by a lorry load of coal and was never the same again. He was only 18. He was rescued but he became mentally ill and unstable. After the accident, the only thing Albi could do was play the piano. The family bought him one of those stand-up honky-tonks that you see in pubs, but in his mental state Albert could play one tune only. One day my grandma walked into the room and asked him not to keep playing the same old boring song. It was getting on her nerves. Albert suddenly snapped. He picked up a big glass ashtray and slammed it straight into his mother's face. From then on, he spent the rest of his life in a mental asylum on Tooting Bec Common.

He terrified the life out of everybody there. My dad used to visit him at weekends. One day, Albi asked if he could get him two gallons of green paint and a brush. Dad thought Albert was just mucking around and forgot all about it. The next time he went Albert was livid.

'Where's the paint, Bill?' he asked. 'You ain't forgot it, have you?'

Albert had a pair of eyes that would have frightened the life out of Hannibal Lecter. So the next time Dad went to visit he made damn sure he had the paint. When Dad returned to the hospital, he found everything in Albert's room painted green – the walls, ceiling, floor, even the bed and its wheels. Nothing at all had been missed. The staff told Dad they had been too scared to stop Albert once he had started.

Before Albert's accident, my dad hadn't been a lot safer in the family house, either. When he was about 19 years old my granddad imposed a curfew.

'When you live under this roof,' he told my dad and Albert, 'be in by midnight. Or else.'

So, of course, the obvious happened. One night my dad came in very late, well beyond the 12 o'clock sharp edict, and his dad was waiting for him.

'Is that you, Billy?' he enquired.

'Yes,' replied my dad, striding purposefully into the hallway.

'Good then,' said Granddad. And without another word he smashed my dad straight in the face with his huge gnarled right fist, knocking him out cold.

Not long after that, a similar incident happened but this time it was my grandfather who was left lying unconscious in the dark. And it didn't end there. Granddad was an extremely proud man. When he came to, he crept into my dad's room and with a club hammer smashed two gaping holes in my dad's knee, crippling him for life. Dad never walked properly again.

But Granddad never laid a finger on Albert. He wouldn't have dared, although he used to give him some verbal. That didn't last for long though. One Saturday when Albert was about 15 he came home and his dad started on him for the last time. Albert said nothing. He just picked up Granddad by the scruff of his neck and lifted him completely off the floor and out the back door. Before Granddad's feet could hit the ground, Albert picked up a screwdriver and drove it through the collar of his dad's coat and into a shed door. There Granddad remained, suspended on the door in the freezing cold for hours. My dad eventually got him down and he was nothing short of polite to Albert ever after. Could you blame him?

Granddad was a typical East London bloke, very hard. Once, gypsies threw human excrement into the hallway of his council flat while he was out and nailed a note to the door demanding money. If he didn't pay up every week, it said, the disgusting deliveries would continue. It was before Albert was born. God knows what would have happened if he'd been around at the time.

Anyway, Granddad went mad. That night he went to the gypsies' campsite with five gallons of petrol and set fire to all their caravans. For his trouble they gave him an horrendous kicking which put him in hospital for two months. His face was an absolute mess. Granddad thought it was worth it. Never again was excrement shoved through his door.

Granddad loved his drink, particularly beer, which eventually cost him his life. One day he was rushed to hospital because of a burst duodenal ulcer and surgeons fought for days to save him. God knows how many stitches they put into his stomach and how many pints of blood they used. Granddad remained in hospital for three weeks and when he was ready to be discharged the doctors gave him a diet sheet. They told him that from now on, he must eat boiled fish only, drink lots of milk and have nothing that would upset his stomach; and he must absolutely never again touch a drop of alcohol. As soon as he was discharged, Granddad marched straight into the nearest pub, downed 17 pints of bitter and died the next day from alcoholic poisoning.

I didn't have any brothers or sisters. My mother had such a bad time with me during childbirth that she was unable to have any more children. However, there was never a dull moment in the Marsh household with 30 or 40 cousins, nephews, uncles and aunts who often came to visit – not all at the same time, I'm glad to say.

Dad's extended family was at least a hundred strong – and strong is the word. There were always rows and punch-ups at Christmas or holiday time. First an uncle would start, or maybe a cousin or two, and it was all off, usually in drink. I am told that a brother-in-law of Dad's was sentenced to 15 years for manslaughter after striking someone in the face with an axe.

In spite of all the violence, I was brought up never to hit a woman. They could hit a man, of course, and often did. It was common to see a bloke being chinned by his missus. My mother used to give my dad some fearful right-handers. He took some terrible provocation but not once did he retaliate. It's something you just don't do. I've taught Jonathan that.

We had to stop seeing my father's family because of all the trouble and fighting. Most of them had been in prison for causing grievous bodily harm and worse. My dad was once jailed for stealing from the docks where he worked.

Don't get me wrong. I think Cockneys are wonderful people by and large. It's often said how way back in the old days you could go out all day with your front door left open and nothing would be touched when you got back. That's what it was like when I was a kid. I'd go from house to house with my pals and people would share what little food they had with you. There was always a cup of tea as soon as you walked through the door. And in spite of all the deprivation, most people I knew were cheerful – always up for a laugh and a giggle. True Cockneys would never steal from you – they might thieve from an outsider but not from one of their own.

One foggy day, my mum answered the door to a lorry driver from the Midlands who had got lost. He asked Mum if she knew if there was a bed and breakfast locally so he could stay the night and start off again the next day. My mum told him there was a place a few streets away but the road was too narrow to park a truck. So the driver asked if he could leave it outside our house overnight. My mum told him he could do what he liked. When the driver returned the following morning, he found his lorry sitting on its axles. It had been broken into and the entire contents removed. Even the wheels had been nicked.

I'm not glorifying violence or condoning it in anyway – far from it. I saw too much as a kid and can only condemn it. In the East End in those days, it was part and parcel of everyday life. I sometimes wonder how it affected me.

I remember in 1969 playing a pre-season friendly for Queens Park Rangers against Glasgow Rangers that ended in a 3–3 draw. It was a fantastic match. Both sides played brilliantly and gave the crowd some great entertainment. Towards the end of the game, Kai Johansson, one of their defenders who had been having a go at me all afternoon, kicked me from behind once too often and we both ended up on the gravel running track that used to surround the Loftus Road pitch in those days. I got up first and I'd had enough. The split second I had to think didn't help me. I was so angry I punched him straight in the face. I knew what I was doing. I knew, too, I was going to be sent off and didn't care. I was out of control. Jimmy Barrett, the QPR trainer and assistant manager, was in the dug-out and saw it all. After I had hit the guy, Jimmy, who was a lovely man, grabbed my arms and held them behind my back. I was going mad. Another Glasgow player came over and stood about two feet away from me snorting with rage. I butted him straight in the face.

When all the fuss had died down, I felt strange. It wasn't me . . . it was as though I was someone else. There were two people lying on the ground in front of me and it was like another person had put them there. I'm not particularly proud of that incident but perhaps it's an example of the effect a violent upbringing can have.

The following week I got a letter from a Glasgow fan telling me that 'some of the boys' were coming down to London to do me and cut up my family. QPR informed the police who immediately put a guard on our house until they thought it was safe.

Curiously, I would never say I had an unhappy childhood. I always had a ball to play with and there were loads of kids around to muck about with. Anyone might think that sort of start in life was terrible and I must have hated it, which I did. I know that sounds contradictory but at the time I wasn't any different from any other kid in the area. We were all in the same boat. We all had the same problems to face. It was a way of life. My friends and neighbours didn't have anything better. It's not until you get out of the gutter that you know any different. It was only later that I realised just what a miserable upbringing I'd had.

My dad was a mad Arsenal fan. After I had played for my local school or club on a Saturday morning, he would take me to watch the Gunners. Rain or shine, we would walk to Highbury through Clissold Park and I would sit on his or an uncle's shoulders to see either the first team or the reserves. I don't think it mattered which to him.

Interestingly, in 1959 one of the biggest names in the game was Wolverhampton Wanderers' centre-half Billy Wright. Billy had just led the Wolves to their second First Division champion-ship in three years and had become the first footballer to win 100 international caps. The England skipper had an unrivalled record playing for his country and had been on the winning side 59 times with 22 draws. He had missed just three of England's 103 post-war internationals and made a record 65 consecutive appearances. He was a proven winner as a player but not capable of achieving that success as a manager at Highbury a few years later.

In spite of Kennedy, I did have something to thank my dad for. He rang West Ham United and told them they should take on his boy, the best kid in London. On top of that, I had just changed schools and my new sports master at Brooke House had connections at West Ham. He put my name forward for a trial. I did really well and they offered me a place in their Under-16 side. My dad was thrilled. Still, he would rather I'd gone to the Arsenal and said so, though why he had phoned West Ham I don't know. It was a strange moment. He had helped get me on to the first rung of the football ladder and I don't remember thanking him. The wounds were too deep. So I shut them out of my mind completely, locked them away and concentrated on one thing – my first game for the Hammers. There was no way family violence was going to burst that bubble.

football? you're having a laugh!

People try to tell you that Stanley Matthews wouldn't get a kick these days but don't you believe it. [He had] the skill and confidence to operate in confined spaces and get past people. Where are the players today who can do this?

Vic Buckingham, Fulham manager 1965–68

Being called a wally isn't exactly an East London term of endearment. But being called one by Wally St Pier was a huge compliment to a kid in the capital in the late 1950s.

Before retiring as West Ham United's chief scout in 1976 after 47 years with the club, Wally was responsible for introducing a stunning array of talent to the Boleyn Ground – Bobby Moore and Martin Peters, for instance, and we all know what happened to them. Inevitably, a few slipped through the net – notably, Jimmy Greaves and Terry Venables who both lived in Wally's manor but were reeled in by Chelsea on the other side of London – but perhaps the bait offered by other clubs was sometimes a bit tastier than West Ham's.

Still, it was well known that there weren't many better judges of young talent in the country, let alone London, than Wally, God rest his soul. So when he invited me to train twice a week in the evenings with West Ham's Under-16 side I was in seventh heaven.

It was the year after Brazil had conquered Europe in the 1958 World Cup. A precocious 17 year old called Pele and the outstanding skills of Didi had given everybody a lesson in tactics. The host nation, Sweden, were made to look positively pedestrian in the final as the South Americans battered them 5–2 to become the first winners of the competition outside their own continent.

The West Ham teams around that time tried to play good football, too. They never reached those Brazilian heights, of course, but they produced fantastic sides. In 1959, the Hammers finished sixth in what was then the First Division after winning the Second Division championship the previous season, a position they have only bettered a couple of times since.

There were some big footballing names around then – Malcolm Allison, Dave Sexton, John Bond, Peter Brabrook, Noel Cantwell, Frank O'Farrell and Malcolm Musgrove all went on to become successful managers and coaches. Two or three senior pros were paid to coach each junior West Ham team twice a week. Left-winger Musgrove looked after my Under-16 side and he went on to excel as an FA staff coach. Even then his footballing knowledge was well respected.

I thought I had really made it. I mean, I was at West Ham's academy. I remember the smell of the liniment at the Grange Farm training ground the first time I walked through the door of the dressing-room. I thought, 'Wow, it doesn't get any better than this. Is this what the pros really do?' I can clearly recall picking up the ball and smelling it. I wanted to take in everything, to absorb it all. Tuesday and Thursday evenings at 5.30 I'd be the first one at the Manor Park training ground and it was marvellous. All the socks, shorts, shirts and ties were neatly laid out. 'Cor,' I thought. 'This is great.' I hadn't seen anything like it.

I got 10 shillings a week expenses, 50p in today's money, and you had to put a claim form in to receive it. It was all so official and proper. I was 15 next birthday and I'd arrived, or so I reckoned. I can remember pulling on the old claret and blue for the first time. It's as if it was yesterday. What a thrill! It was an incredible feeling, especially as I had spent all my few years of life dreaming about it.

Harry Redknapp was in my side at the time. Brian Dear and Johnny Sissons, who also became big names at Upton Park, were there too. I scored plenty of goals with them and we won loads of games.

After about 10 months, Wally called me in to his office. Ridiculously, I thought it might be to say that I was being promoted to the first team. Bobby Moore had been elevated six or seven months earlier. When Wally told me that West Ham were not renewing my amateur status, I was devastated, crushed.

'Rodney,' he said, 'we're going to let you go. We believe there's a boy in our youth side who will become a better player than you. So we've decided to sign him instead and there's no room for you.'

Now I can see the dilemma Wally faced. The boy was Geoff Hurst, later to be knighted for services to football and the man who hit a glorious hat-trick in England's 1966 World Cup victory over West Germany. We later became good pals, as did our wives. Geoff's a smashing guy and he was one of the best strikers England have produced.

Walking home that day, I really felt as if I was out on the cobbles. I hadn't even met the manager, Ted Fenton. As it turned out, his days at Upton Park were also numbered. But I picked myself up. Rejection can be hard to take but I wasn't going to hang around moping. If you believe in yourself, and I did, you've got to keep plugging away. It's what I'd tell any kid today. Soon I was my old chirpy self again, especially after going back to Alexander Boys' and banging in a bucket load of goals for them.

Six months later, just before my 16th birthday, Fulham scout Bill Brown spotted me. Bill was an honest old pro with trusting eyes, the kind of man you warm to instantly. When Fulham offered me the chance to become one of their Craven Cottage groundstaff boys, I leapt at the chance.

For a start, it was the club Johnny Haynes, my boyhood hero, played for. He was the Fulham and England captain for heaven's sake, the golden boy of British football, the Brylcreem boy before David Beckham was born, and probably the first footballer to be used in a big endorsement or advertisement.

I don't think it's appreciated how big Johnny was then. The other day I was talking to some people, who weren't that young, and I had to explain who he was. I couldn't believe it. So let me put it simply – Johnny was David Beckham, Patrick Vieira and Paul Scholes rolled into one, and that's no exaggeration.

Johnny always wore the No. 10 shirt, which was my favourite number, too. From the start I was determined to emulate him. He had sublime skills. He could pass a ball any distance with pinpoint accuracy, score regularly, tackle, beat people and organise everything. In fact, there wasn't anything he couldn't do. Johnny stood head and shoulders above any other player in those days. I stood in awe.

So I dropped out of school before taking my full GCE examinations, even though I'd done well in the mock tests a year earlier.

The previous season, Fulham had finished 10th in the First Division, four places above West Ham and three in front of Arsenal, as I reminded my dad even though I was a bit of a Gunners nut myself. Incidentally, just to show how the game's been turned on its head since then, Burnley had finished champions that year with a cracking side managed by a bloke called Harry Potts. Harry never got tired of telling his players to keep possession, play football and enjoy themselves. That bit of advice wouldn't be out of place today. Other top clubs were Wolves, West Brom, Sheffield Wednesday, Bolton Wanderers and Preston.

At Fulham, the manager was a former player, Bedford Jezzard. Frank Osborne, the general manager, was in charge of everything other than the team and ruled the place with a rod of iron. He had a huge boardroom-sized desk from which he rarely looked up when he spoke. The only people who got that kind of respect were Frank and the old-time music-hall comedian Tommy Trinder, who was the chairman – and, of course, Johnny Haynes. That's the sort of reverence he was held in at Fulham, and everywhere else come to that.

As I was on my way to SW6, over in Belfast at Lisnasharragh Immediate School, George Best's genius had already attracted the interest of Manchester United, just as Sir Matt Busby was returning to full duties following the Munich air crash that cost the lives of eight Busby Babes. Terry Venables had not long joined Chelsea as one of Ted Drake's Ducklings, and, as far as I know, hadn't yet tried to take over Stamford Bridge like he did everywhere else he went. Malcolm Allison was beginning his management career with non-league Bath City after having a lung removed because of tuberculosis. Bobby Moore, England's youth team captain, had taken his place in the Hammers' defence. Another hero of mine, Denis Law, was about to be transferred to Manchester City from Huddersfield for a British record of £55,000 – still wearing national health glasses. The previous year, Elton John's cousin Roy Dwight had been carried off with a broken leg playing right-wing for Nottingham Forest in their 2–1 FA Cup final win over Luton. Legendary Tottenham Hotspur boss Bill Nicholson was in his second season in charge at White Hart Lane. Bill's first game at the helm had been a mind-boggling 10–4 battering of Everton. All our paths crossed memorably over the years.

Things were looking up on the home front. My dad, having been poor for most of his life, had a real stroke of luck just before I went to Craven Cottage. For years he had religiously filled in our landlord's football pools coupon every week. One Saturday, Dad was checking the coupon and found the landlord had eight draws, which was one of the best things you could get. Then he heard a radio announcement saying that anyone with such luck should urgently send a telegram claim. It could be a bumper payout. Dad went straight to our landlord to tell him the good news. He reckoned there would be a couple of thousand pounds to come, which was a tidy sum.

The landlord, an old Jewish guy, duly fired off his telegram and a reply came back the next day telling him that he had won the treble chance dividend of £38,602, which was an absolute fortune 40 years ago. It was heart-attack city! Today that amount would be worth well over a million pounds, or more. It was like winning the lottery. You could have bought 15 houses with that sort of cash.

After a few days, the landlord came to see my dad to thank him.

'Billy,' he said, 'I'd just like to say how grateful I am to you for all you've done for me. Here. As a gesture of appreciation, take the extra two pounds from my winnings.'

Dad was gutted. From that moment on, he never spoke to the landlord again, or filled in another pools coupon for him.

Not long afterwards, the landlord died suddenly and left my dad the house in which we lived. In his will the landlord said that he had felt bad about the way he had treated my father and wanted to make amends. So Dad could have the whole flipping house, including the other two flats, lock, stock and barrel.

Dad was stunned. He was now a landlord himself, something he never dreamed would happen. Eventually, he sold the house and we moved to Edmonton, which was a step up for us at the time. When we got there, Dad had a telephone installed. That was considered a real luxury.

If training with West Ham was exciting, joining Fulham was nothing short of intoxicating. The only drawback was that Craven Cottage was a long way from Edmonton. I was lucky because Derek Lampe, one of Fulham's centre-halves, and Frank Penn, the club's trainer, lived in the area, too. They took it in turns to pick me up and drive me to the ground and back.

There were eight of us groundstaff boys, or YTS trainees as they are called now, at Craven Cottage. Supervised by groundsman Jackie Gordon, we had to sweep the whole ground including the terraces, clean the kit room, the press box and the bars, and wash all the towels. We also had to polish the players' boots. My first job on my first day was to clean Johnny Haynes' boots after he had played for England in a 4–2 win over Spain at Wembley. The 100,000 capacity crowd had been calling his name all night long. But I called him 'Mr Haynes'.

I was so thrilled to be touching the hallowed Wembley turf that was on Johnny's boots that I emptied a box of Bryant & May matches and carefully inserted a piece of grass as a souvenir. I took the box home that night and kept it for ages with the medals I had won as a kid.

It was a laugh a minute at Fulham. I got £5 10s (£5 50p) a week and £2 if the youth team won, but I would have signed for nothing just for the entertainment value. This is typical of what went on there on an almost daily basis. One morning Johnny Haynes had to report to the medical room, Frankie Penn's domain, after an earlier England midweek international. Johnny had suffered a dead leg and needed urgent treatment to be fit for Fulham's league game on Saturday. He hobbled up to the medical room and knocked on Frankie's door, but there was no answer. Mysteriously, the door was locked.

Johnny was puzzled. He'd seen Frank go into the room on his way to explain the situation to the boss 15 minutes earlier. So he knocked again. There was still no reply. Now Johnny was getting a bit wound up and he started to bang on the door. Then he kicked it and shouted, 'Frank, Frank, let me in. It's Johnny. I've got to have treatment right away.' The room was as quiet as a grave.

Johnny lost his temper, 'Frankie. It's Johnny Haynes. Can

you hear me? Frank. For heaven's sake, let me in. What's going on in there?'

Furiously, Johnny continued to hammer and push on the door. The commotion got louder and louder and Johnny's language became unprintable. Finally, he took a few paces back and threw himself at the door. That did the trick and it flew open, sending Frank, who had been behind it, sprawling to the floor. Johnny stumbled into the room and couldn't believe what was in front of his eyes. There on the treatment table lay a greyhound with a bruised hindquarter that Frank had been working on. Johnny nearly exploded. Here was Frank giving preference to a dog owned by Fulham forward Charlie Mitten over the Fulham and England captain and the biggest name in the game at the time. What made the greyhound more important than Johnny was that it was due to run in the one o'clock race that afternoon at Stamford Bridge, carrying with it Frank's and Charlie's hard-earned cash. Classic!

Not only did I clean Johnny Haynes' boots, I was also his caddy, which was a privilege. Johnny was a smashing golfer. In those days, before Cup ties we'd go to an hotel on the seafront in Worthing, Sussex, for four or five days to prepare. We'd train in the morning, play golf in the afternoon, then play cards in the evening, gambling among ourselves. Full-back Jim Langley used to bring a wicker hamper full of all the paraphernalia – cards, dice, roulette wheel and even eyeshades and armbands.

One afternoon we were on the local golf course. Haynes was playing with a half-back called Eddie Lowe and a couple of other players, and there's me trundling along with Johnny's bag. Eddie was a smashing bloke but a bit of a moaner. He'd grumble about everything from breakfast on, giving everyone earache. After a few holes, Eddie started – his shoes didn't fit right, the sun was in his eyes and the wind was wrong. On and on he went. Finally, he reckoned the group in front was playing too slowly. At the next tee, Eddie urged Johnny to take his shot before the foursome in front had completed the hole.

'Go on, Johnny,' said Eddie. 'We'll be here all night if you don't get a move on.'

'I can't go yet,' replied Haynes. 'They haven't finished putting. It's not safe.'

Eddie became more and more irritable.

'Don't be daft, John. They're two hundred and seventy yards away at least. You'll never get near them in a month of Sundays.'

Reluctantly, just to stop Eddie's grizzling, Johnny teed off – and unleashed a shot that Tiger Woods would have been proud of. The ball screamed down the fairway straight as an arrow. Shading our eyes from the sun, we could just pick out Derek Lampe putting from about 15 feet from the next hole. Then suddenly he dropped to the floor as if he'd been struck with a bullet. Johnny's shot had hit Derek right on the back of the head, knocking him out cold. We all rushed to help him but poor old Lampey was unconscious for several minutes. Not only was he out of Saturday's game, he didn't play again for six weeks. No wonder we didn't progress to the next round!

I always felt a bit bad for Johnny. He played 56 times for England, 22 as captain, but his career was cut short. He was in a car crash just after the 1962 World Cup tournament and although he recovered sufficiently to play at club level again, and even managed Fulham until 1970 before leaving to play in South Africa, he was never the same.

When I look back at the years I spent with Fulham it's strange. I can remember some sensational games because we were capable of playing some great stuff. Yet the record books show we were always battling to stay in the First Division. We weren't often heavily beaten but lost a lot of games by the odd goal. When that happened, Tommy Trinder would still tell jokes over the ground's tannoy system. There always seemed to be a carnival atmosphere and it didn't take me long to get involved in some of the pantomimes that made it such a joy to be at Craven Cottage.

I was always pushing the envelope out – testing authority. All footballers do it, even today. They push and push a situation or a person to see how much they can get away with. Perhaps I went a bit too far at times and I guess I was lucky not to be sacked in my first year. I was always getting into fights and was generally a bit of a nuisance.

There was one spectacular punch-up with left-back Freddie Callaghan after I had been there for a few months. Freddie tackled me from behind in a five-a-side training game and gave me a kick. I reacted angrily and we squared up to each other. Then we had an old-fashioned stand-up knuckle with neither of us giving ground. Everyone looked on in astonishment. Afterwards, as so often happens, Fred and I became very good friends. Our reward at the time, though, was to be called before Frank Osborne who told us that a repeat performance would earn us the sack.

I didn't take it too seriously. I should have because in those days footballers were a dime a dozen. Every First Division club had 10 or 15 good kids. Today they are few and far between.

My next fight was with a lad called Micky Jones who hid my watch. I gave him a right clump. Then I had a bit of fisticuffs with Tony Goodgame, which got me a final warning from Mr Osborne. It's true that I was always very remorseful after being reprimanded, full of guilt. But somehow I couldn't stop going back for more. I didn't seem to be able to help myself. I was a natural maverick.

Then Fulham signed a really skilful kid called Stevie Earle who became a terrific player for the club. In those days, the groundstaff boys had an initiation ceremony for new recruits. They would be thrown in an ice-cold bath and then painted with the whitewash that was used for the pitch lines. I'd been through it myself when I arrived, and they'd used a wire brush to remove the paint from my privates! On this occasion, I was out of order. After giving Steve the treatment, we dragged him outside where I tied him stark naked to the stand. It was a bitterly cold day and he was left there for three hours.

Again, predictably, I was called in to see Mr Osborne. This time I was left in no doubt that a recurrence would see me on my bike. Fortunately, Frank got the message across. If he hadn't, I would have missed knowing some of the game's truly great characters – George Cohen, Alan Mullery, Graham Leggett, Bobby Keetch and Tosh Chamberlain for instance.

Jimmy Hill was there, too, the man every professional footballer today should personally thank for getting the maximum wage rule abolished. Jimmy, as chairman of the Professional Footballers Association, achieved that in my first year at Fulham and I can remember him asking us lads to support the strike that he had threatened. It didn't come to that because in January of 1961, after a meeting between the League and the PFA at the Ministry of Labour, the League agreed to scrap the contract binding players to their clubs for life, so ending 'soccer slavery' and the £20 a week wage limit.

Tommy Trinder had always joked that if that happened, he would make Johnny the first £100 a week footballer, never expecting to pay up. Nonetheless, Trinder kept his word and that led to a famous story that has frequently been misquoted over the years. Just after the maximum wage was abolished, Frank Osborne called Johnny in to give him the rise that the chairman had promised. There were no agents in those days. Players negotiated their own salary directly with the manager or chairman.

Before seeing the general manager, Haynes had promised his good mate Maurice Cook, Fulham's bustling centre-forward, that he would tell him what money he had been offered so Maurice would know what to ask for himself. After the meeting, Maurice was waiting in the corridor when Johnny, grinning like a Cheshire cat, came out of the office.

'How did you do?' asked Maurice.

'Great. One hundred pounds a week in the season and eighty

pounds during the summer,' replied Johnny.

Armed with that knowledge, Maurice was straight in to see what the club's offer to him would be. He was rather peeved when Frank Osborne said the club could only afford to give him £60 a week in the winter and £40 during the off-season.

'But I've just spoken to Johnny outside and he tells me you've given him eighty pounds,' protested Maurice. Frank Osborne stood up and looked Cooky straight in the face.

'Look Maurice, Johnny is captain of Fulham, captain of England and the best player in the country by miles,' he said.

'Not in the summer he's not,' fumed Maurice.

Haynes had rejected the chance to play for Tottenham to join Fulham because Tosh Chamberlain, his best friend and an amazing personality, was already at Craven Cottage. I remember watching the first team play Manchester United one Saturday and Johnny hitting a glorious 60-yard pass out to Chamberlain on the wing. Tosh wasn't watching the ball. He was far too busy arguing with one of the spectators, something he regularly did. Johnny was livid. He immediately ran over to Chamberlain and had a furious bust-up with his mate as the game went on without them.

There is another marvellous story about Tosh. His wife woke up in the middle of the night.

'Trevor,' she said nervously. 'I think there's someone in the house. Go and check that everything is all right, will you?'

Reluctantly, Tosh crept out to the landing and peered into the darkness.

'Hello?' he whispered. 'I don't know who you are, but take what you want. Just leave me alone!'

In the late fifties and early sixties, Craven Cottage was stacked with hilarious people from the chairman down. One cold and frosty morning we had a practice game to see what a South African boy called Eddie Abrahams could do. He had flown in from Johannesburg a few days before. But when the game was due to kick off, Abrahams couldn't be found. The boss, Bedford Jezzard, was getting more and more agitated and I was finally dispatched to search the ground for Eddie. I hunted for more than half an hour, but I couldn't find him anywhere. He had disappeared into thin air.

The game was eventually played minus our South African and I went on with my job washing the training gear. Then, when I opened the door of one of the large ovens which was used to dry the clothes, I saw the whites of a pair of eyes staring back at me. Having not long left 90 degree temperatures, Eddie just couldn't tolerate a London winter's day and in desperation had climbed into the oven for some warmth, not caring about why he'd made the journey in the first place.

We had a reserve goalkeeper called Ken Hewkins. Ken wasn't on an awful lot of money and to supplement his income he worked behind the bar of a local pub in the evenings. Around lunchtime one Saturday, Jezzard rang Ken and told him he was in the first team that afternoon. Tony Mecedo, the regular keeper, had woken up with influenza and was unable to play.

'OK, boss,' mumbled Ken.

'I can't hear you, son. Speak up. Oh never mind. Listen, go straight to the ground and change,' ordered Bedford.

Ken was sitting in the dressing-room completely unfazed when the boss walked in to give his usual pre-game talk. Bedford looked around the room, spotted Hewkins and his jaw immediately dropped. Ken's face was a mess. Both his eyes were closed and his lips were swollen from a fight he had had in the pub the night before.

Another time, we played a reserve game against Charlton at Craven Cottage. There must have been about eight spectators – seven in the stand and one old guy on the terraces behind the goal. The match kicked off and you could hear this one bloke in a booming voice giving Ken some rotten stick. Hewkins you're a this and Hewkins you're a that echoed all around the ground.

After about 20 minutes, a Charlton defender hoofed the ball from his own half into our penalty area and we watched in horror as the ball bounced leisurely into an unguarded goal. Ken in his studded boots was slipping and sliding on the concrete terraces, exchanging punches with his abuser.

In another reserve match, this time against Birmingham, Ken had been injured and I volunteered to take his place. I'd not been between the posts for long when they got a corner. When the ball came over, for some inexplicable reason I tried to bicycle kick it over the bar instead of catching it. Unfortunately, I slammed the ball into my own net. Everyone roared with laughter, except the manager of course. After the game was over, Bedford Jezzard was furious.

'What the hell were you trying to do,' he fumed.

'Entertain the punters,' I replied.

'If I wanted players to do that,' Bedford said, 'I would have signed some clowns in the first place.'

So I told him, 'Why bother? You've got a first team full of them already.'

When he walked away, I was positive he was smiling.

Pre-season training was just as funny. To get us fit after the summer excesses we used to run from Craven Cottage through Bishop's Park and over Putney Bridge. Then we would go right up the hill to Richmond Park and do a full training programme before jogging back. The whole session would take about two and a half hours.

The first time I did it as a 17 year old, I sprinted off with another couple of young lads, eager to impress. After the session at Richmond Park had finished, Bedford Jezzard ordered everyone back in their own time. I dashed off like a hare, determined to be the first one back and really catch the boss's eye. Out in front of all the first-team members and racing along the Lower Richmond Road, I turned around and when I couldn't see anyone behind me I thought I'd out-sprinted everybody and was very pleased with myself. Then a bus pulled up alongside and on board was Jim Langley and most of the first-team squad putting their thumbs up and laughing at me. They beat me back by about 15 minutes and I got a right telling off from the trainer because he was sure I was last back because I'd stopped off for a drink on the way. You couldn't take anything seriously then. Can you imagine Manchester United players doing that?

I eventually broke into the first team, aged 19, on 23 March 1963 against Aston Villa at Craven Cottage. I took the place of Johnny Haynes, who was injured, and proudly wore his No. 10 shirt. I would have given almost anything to have made my first appearance for Fulham alongside him.

No player forgets his debut, especially when you score the winning goal. It was a right-foot volley from a George Cohen cross in the 61st minute, similar to the Di Canio 1999–2000 goal of the season, only better!

I got a terrific press with the headlines screaming: 'It's Marsh's day – now he's back in the shadows'. Everybody knew that next week when Johnny was fit I'd be back in the stiffs. Still, Fulham had to find a place for me somewhere after I'd bagged 40 goals for the reserves. So I got the No. 8 shirt. The position had been vacated by Jimmy Hill who had left to manage Coventry.

Then came a major setback. Not long after breaking into the first team, I was seriously injured in a game against Leicester at Filbert Street and was told that I would never play again.

In the early 1960s, the Foxes were a force to be reckoned with and the previous season there had been talk of them doing the double. They finally finished fourth, their highest placing since the Second World War, and were beaten 3–1 by Manchester United in the FA Cup final.

They had some tremendous players including legendary goal-keeper Gordon Banks, Frank McLintock, who later led Arsenal to their famous 1971 double, and Mike Springfellow, one of the bravest wingers I've ever seen. They also had a determined hardman defender called John Sjoberg.

Towards the end of the match, I beat Sjoberg to a cross and headed the winning goal, but he caught me with a late challenge on the side of the head, fracturing my jaw and skull. The result was horrific and I've been deaf in one ear ever since. I didn't even see him coming.

I was unconscious for five or six minutes before being stretchered off the pitch. When Frankie Penn got me to the dressing-room I could not stand up and was rushed to Leicester Infirmary where I was detained overnight. Bedford Jezzard stayed with me and brought me back on the train the following day. Even my dad was concerned and it showed when he met us at the station.

I had tests in London hospitals for more than a week but I couldn't keep my balance and was disorientated. I was so concussed that if I laid my head down, the room would not stop spinning. I had to sit up all the time and couldn't stop vomiting.

Eventually, I began to feel a bit better but it was about three or four weeks before I realised I had lost the hearing in my left ear. The doctors thought it was caused by the concussion and that it might return in time, but it never did. I stayed at home for months. However hard I tried, I couldn't keep my balance and would fall over if I stood for more than a few minutes.

Six months later I went to another ear, nose and throat specialist who discovered that a bone splinter from my jaw had severed a nerve to my ear. It was an extraordinarily painful injury. Also, because of the severity of the concussion, the fluid in the semi-circular canals of my ears, which controls the equilibrium, had drained. I had to wait until my body naturally replaced it before I could walk properly again.

Fulham sent me to the local hospital, St Stephen's, and specialists there told me I would never play again. I refused to believe them. For some reason, I knew I would make a comeback.

That's how determined I was to be a footballer.

I was out for almost 10 months. During that time, I just sat around drawing, which had been a hobby of mine since I was about 13. I studied at the Geffrye School of Art in Stoke Newington, a night-class school, for two years from the age of 14. Now it came in handy because all I could do was sit around and sketch. I copied pictures by Chagall, the German renaissance painter Holbein and landscape artist Gainsborough. I also drew still life. At least it stopped me brooding. I had just signed a three-year contract with a two-year option but, as any player will tell you, that's not much consolation when you've been seriously injured.

I learned the techniques of sketching and oil and watercolour painting at night school but never had the drive to continue with it; other things became higher priorities in my life. From time to time I sketched portraits of different characters including Picasso, Oliver Cromwell and Shakespeare. My favourite was the Picasso and I can't believe that I gave it away. I can't even remember who it was I gave it to. Later on in my life, I studied the William Alexander method of landscape oil painting and still occasionally dust off the old palette when I'm back in Tampa and spend a few days painting. However, in recent years all of my paintings have been unfinished. Maybe I should cut off my ear and send it to a prostitute for inspiration!

My interest extended beyond trying my hand at it, and in addition to in-depth reading about all my favourite artists, I began collecting more and more pieces of art. As my earnings increased, I was able to buy some works by the artists I admired the most, including some Dali lithographs, some north-western Indian original prints and several busts including one of William Shakespeare.

Eventually, my fitness returned. I went on an army rehabilitation training course, which helped improve my balance. As part of the treatment, nurses held me up while I walked on special boards. When I first went back to Fulham, I tried to walk along the white pitch lines but I leaned to one side and fell over after 10 yards. That's a scary feeling I'll always remember, but I never once doubted that I would be back. When I started jogging, the feeling was wonderful – but not as good as proving the doctors wrong when I eventually returned to full training. The biggest test was still to come. Could I head a ball? I can only describe the first time I tried as traumatic, but in my first few games back I quickly learned how to protect myself with my arms. I only wish I'd done it a year earlier.

As far as I know, I don't think there has been anyone in the history of the game who has played at Premiership level completely deaf in one ear.

Not long after getting back to full fitness I met my wife, Jean, in a jazz club in Manor Park when I was out one night with a few of the other Fulham youngsters. I was 20 at the time, footloose and fancy free, and I plucked up the courage to speak to her and ask her to dance. She was from Barking and had never heard of me, and she was the nicest girl I had ever met. We exchanged numbers, I called her and that was the start of our relationship.

The following season, 1964–65, I switched to the centre-forward's No. 9 shirt and had a great year playing alongside Johnny Haynes and scoring against Manchester United, Arsenal and Spurs. In fact, I played the whole season in the first team.

At 21, I was very highly principled about what was right and what was wrong, always an outcast and a rebel, very much a 'today is a good day to die' type of guy. If I felt I was in the right, I was prepared to go to the wall and suffer the consequences. My dad had frequently preached to me, 'You can do what you want in this world. Just as long as you are prepared to suffer the consequences.' And that's the way I have always conducted my life.

That attitude cost me my job at Fulham in the end. Bedford Jezzard had left the club after Alan Mullery was sold to Spurs behind his back, clearly undermining his position. Bedford, just 37 at the time, resigned to run a pub. Fulham missed him a lot more than he missed football. Vic Buckingham took over. He had been a White Hart Lane wing-half during his playing career and cut his managerial teeth at Bradford before joining West Bromwich Albion. He took them to victory in the FA Cup in his first year. After leaving the Hawthorns he moved to Amsterdam and led Ajax to the Dutch title, which obviously went to his head because when he came to Fulham he spoke in a ridiculous half Dutch half English accent. You couldn't make it up.

Buckingham had a reputation as a deep and original thinker. His theories on the game were based on his experiences coaching Oxford University. I ask you! He changed everything at Craven Cottage for the sake of it and in three dismal years in charge the only thing he did of significance was sign Allan Clarke from Walsall. Amazingly, he went on to take charge at Ethnikos in Greece and at Spanish clubs Barcelona and Seville.

Buckingham considered himself to be one of football's intellectuals, but all the players thought he was a clown. 'Tricky Vicky', as he was called, would turn up at training in tweeds with a big white handkerchief hanging out of his top pocket like some eccentric.

One day he called a few players together on the pitch and told us, 'I think you all need to be aware that to improve you've got to be lighter on your feet.' Then right there in front of George Cohen, Bobby Keetch and me, he started tap-dancing like Fred Astaire as we looked on in amazement. When he had finished he said, 'When you can do this you'll be much better players!'

Well, I couldn't control myself and burst out laughing. Keetchy just shook his head slowly and said, 'What a prat!' The next day, Bobby was sold to Queens Park Rangers.

Things at Fulham went from bad to worse. I couldn't tolerate what was going on under Buckingham and didn't hesitate to tell him so, on more than one occasion. Finally, we weren't even talking to one another and he refused to select me.

I shouldn't have been surprised, therefore, when in March 1966, Buckingham called me into his office and told me that the club had had an offer of £15,000 from QPR to follow Keetch to Loftus Road. It was a pittance. I was shocked. It was the only bid that Fulham had received and I couldn't believe it. I had been knocking in goals left, right and centre for a First Division side in front of crowds of over 30,000 a week and the one club that wanted me was two divisions below and attracted gates of around 8,000.

When you've shared a dressing-room with the likes of Haynes, Cohen and Mullery, dropping down that far can be a major cultural shock, especially when you're 22. When I told Jean that Queens Park Rangers had come in for me she thought I was moving to Scotland! I reckoned the way I was going, I'd be out of the League in no time at all.

But as soon as I realised that I wasn't wanted at Craven Cottage, my attitude was bollocks to them. All I wanted to be was a footballer. I wanted to be happy doing the only thing I knew how. I couldn't be sure that I would be happy at Loftus Road, but I was sure I wasn't going to be happy with Fulham any more. So when I thought about it, Rangers didn't seem such a bad move. For a start, I'd get a raise. I was on about £20 a week at Craven Cottage but QPR's manager, Alec Stock, had promised me an extra fiver; and I would be back with my old pal Bobby Keetch and another former team-mate, Jim Langley.

On top of that, Rangers had just acquired Les Allen, the father of Clive, whom I later discovered possessed one of the best footballing brains around. I knew they had some decent home-grown talents, too, speedy winger Roger Morgan for instance. So not everything was doom and gloom. Lying in third place, 10 points behind Hull City and Millwall, Rangers had some games in hand and with a little bit of luck there was an outside chance of promotion, or so Alec Stock told me.

I knew I had the skill to beat defenders in close situations, score goals and give the punters what they wanted. What impressed me most was that Alec told me straightaway he would mould Rangers around me. All I had to do was go on the pitch and perform.

I never once doubted my ability, just my application. I couldn't be bothered with managers whom I considered useless. I wasn't very coachable in those days and reckoned I knew better than a lot of other people did. More often than not, I was right.

CHAPTER 3

rod-nee, rod-nee

Winning isn't everything. It's the only thing.

Vince Lombardi, coach of American
football team Green Bay Packers 1959–67

Jim Gregory was a villain. When I say villain, I mean it in the nicest possible way. If Jim was here today, I am sure he would not mind me describing him like that, God rest his soul.

He had joined the board of directors at Queens Park Rangers in November 1964 after rejecting a similar invitation from Fulham. Five months later, Mr Gregory was chairman. Sometimes I wonder how different my career might have been if he had chosen to go to Craven Cottage.

Jim had two sons and he treated me like a third. From my very first day at Loftus Road, he went out of his way to look after me, just like he did his own family. Heaven help anybody – and I mean *anybody* – who crossed him on that score.

Jim frequently took me into his confidence. Over the six fabulous years I spent at Rangers, we had many private and personal conversations. One afternoon the phone rang in his office. I heard his end of the conversation and he told me afterwards that the call was from a notorious figure of the underworld, which in itself was not particularly unusual. Through his motor businesses and other interests he had acquired many diverse friends and acquaintances, some enemies, plus an enormous amount of wealth. Yet even he was taken aback when the sinister voice told him that one of his young sons, who were aged around 10 at the time, was about to be kidnapped and only a hefty ransom could avert the danger. Jim wasn't having any of it.

'OK,' he hissed into the telephone. 'Do what you've got to do. But you're not getting a penny. Just remember, if anything happens to either of my kids, you're dead!'

He was fuming. You could tell he meant it. In spite of his brusque exterior, he could be emotional. But no one pushed Jim Gregory around. He believed that you should always stand up to bullies. That day he challenged some of the hardest men that were around at the time. His sons were never touched. They knew big Jim Gregory was a man of his word.

Jim threw a protective cloak around me when I got to Rangers. Nobody could say a bad word in my direction when he was around. I don't know why Jim thought so much of me but he did, and it showed. Perhaps it was the way I played. Who knows? I've never experienced a chairman like him before or since, and I am grateful that we had such a special relationship.

My first training session with Rangers was a breath of fresh air, particularly after Vic Buckingham's posturing. Everybody was so cheerful.

My debut was away to Peterborough on a rainy Saturday in March 1966. The ball was being bombed over my head from penalty area to penalty area and I thought, 'What the hell am I doing here?' But the next week it was like being on a different planet. I made my first home appearance against Millwall, who with Hull City were favourites for promotion. It was a game Rangers had to win to stay in the promotion hunt. I can still hear the fans. They were fantastic.

I got off to a flyer and scored in the fourth minute of a competitive tussle that we eventually won 6–1. Alex Stepney, in goal for Millwall, said that up to that point it was the biggest mauling he'd had. He didn't have many bad days after that, spending most of his career with Manchester United. I couldn't have asked for a better first performance in front of the Loftus Road fans.

We had 4–1 victories in the next two games but we weren't quite ready to go up and finished the season 12 points behind Millwall. Surprisingly, nobody was despondent – a bit disappointed maybe, but not down. In fact, I can remember leaving the training ground for the summer break with everybody already excited about returning. In football, unless you've won something, that's rare.

Football has changed a lot. In my day, I always took a summer job to subsidise my income. There were internationals who did the same, even after the maximum wage was abolished in 1961. One year while I was at Fulham, I got a job in a factory stacking cans, but walked out after the supervisor kept telling me I wasn't doing it properly. He had such a boring voice I can still hear it today. It drove me mad. I mean, how many ways can you put a can on a shelf? Only a month or so earlier, I had been playing against Manchester United in front of 60,000 people and this pillock was bossing me about over a tin can. I can't imagine even a Third Division, let alone a Premiership, player stacking cans in the summer to make ends meet.

From then on, in the close season I went to work with my dad as a labourer in the docks. I did that every year until 1965 when Jean and I decided to tour Europe to see if we were compatible. We spent May, June and July in Switzerland, France and Italy. We lived in Italy for 10 weeks. When we came back, I proposed and we were married in March of 1967.

Before the 1966–67 season kicked off, Jim Gregory had given me a flat in a block he owned in Roehampton, south west London, as part of my deal. The building overlooked the spot where Marc Bolan, the rock star, was later tragically killed in a car crash. It became our first home after we were married and it was great because Bobby Keetch and his wife Jan lived below us. Bobby shared my love of art. He had some antiques and paintings. Jean and I would often go round for dinner and we'd end up spending hours discussing his art collection.

That season began on a tidal wave of passion. England had beaten West Germany 4–2 in the World Cup final at Wembley in July. When I reported back for training you could feel the buzz straightaway. We all knew that something special was about to happen to us, too.

It took us a couple of games to get going. After a home draw and an away defeat, we were languishing in 22nd spot, but then we really took off. Three games later I hit my first hat-trick for Rangers in a 4–0 win over Middlesbrough and we went on to score 35 goals in our first 10 games. By November, we were top and that's where we stayed, losing just once on the way to the Third Division championship.

It was our performances in the League Cup that really made everyone sit up. In the first round we faced Colchester. Sir Stanley Rous, then President of FIFA, had switched on the Essex club's new floodlights at Layer Road. I turned them off with a four-goal burst in a 5–0 win.

In the fourth-round home tie, we beat First Division Leicester 4–2. They included internationals Gordon Banks, Derek Dougan and Peter Rodriguez in their ranks and their two goals flattered them.

In the next round I scored twice when we beat Carlisle United, who were top of the Second Division. That put us into a two-legged semi-final against another First Division side, Birmingham City. In the first leg at St Andrews, in front of a 34,000 crowd, we were in no mood to be overawed despite Barry Bridges giving the Blues a 1–0 lead. In the second half, we simply played Birmingham off the park. I got a quick equaliser and Roger Morgan, Mark Lazarus and Les Allen gave us a memorable 4–1 victory.

In the second leg at Loftus Road, in front of our biggest home gate of the season, I hit another two in a 3–1 win. That gave us a 7–2 aggregate result, and a first ever Wembley Cup final place for a Third Division club. I don't think anyone was sober for days.

Today, a club would prepare for a game like that by going to a luxury training complex in Spain, or some grand place in the English countryside. Alec Stock said the club could not afford it, so Rangers got ready for the biggest game in their history by training at Ruislip, as usual.

The night before the final, Alec untied QPR's purse strings and booked us into an old hotel in central London to calm us down because he thought we were getting too excited. The place was just around the corner from Lancaster Gate and it was no Ritz or Savoy. Actually, it could well have passed for a boarding house. When we were told that we would be spending the night before the final in a West End hotel, Bobby Keetch burst out laughing. 'You're having a laugh,' he roared.

The whole lot of us went out to dinner with the chairman and Alec, and had a few beers. During the evening Keetchy, who was in the 22-man squad but not in the side, had a brainwave. He was the perfect character to have around in those situations. Not long after we had finished the meal, Bobby sneaked off and phoned a Mr Fix-it friend of his who organised a couple of young ladies to come to his hotel room later in the night for a bit of, well, let's just say light entertainment. On top of that, he ordered in a crate of champagne. The rumour spread like wildfire – 'exhibition in 401' was the shout.

Bobby thought that just a few of the Rangers' likely lads would join him to see the strippers give a late-night show. No chance! When the girls turned up at the appointed hour, Bobby was astonished to find all but two of the players marching into his tiny room. It was comical. They were on top of the wardrobe, on the windowsill and even sitting on the television. 'Men Behaving Badly' wasn't in it – and no one was disappointed with the show, which got a bit raunchy. No, I'm not going to name the two players who didn't show up; they were miserable bastards anyway. Who says I can't keep a secret!

The performance, which had started at 11, didn't end until gone one in the morning and eventually all the lads drifted off still clutching their glasses. I don't think Alec ever found out about our party. If he did, he never said a word to us. That's what made him such a brilliant manager. If he had known, I'm sure he would not have done anything. The last thing Alec would have wanted was damage to the harmony of the team. Personally, I feel those sort of situations can help build team spirit, of which we certainly had plenty. Somehow, though, I can't see Sir Alex Ferguson or Arsene Wenger taking a leaf out of Alec's book.

We drove to Wembley the next day and got there about an hour before the kick-off, like some park team. I can still see Alec getting off the team bus in the navy blue jacket and light blue socks that he wore to every game. A lot of players have idiosyncrasies like that. Some get very nervous if they don't follow a certain pattern when they are preparing for a game. I've never been nervous before a match in my life. Let's get on with it was my attitude.

Our opponents were the holders, West Bromwich Abion, who the previous year had beaten West Ham in the last two-legged League Cup final. This time, Albion had beaten the Hammers 6–2 on aggregate in their semi-final. They were a very useful First Division outfit and had some excellent players in former Rangers winger Clive Clark, Ally 'Bomber' Brown and Bobby Hope, who was a stylish midfield artist.

They also had Jeff Astle, a bustling centre-forward who, three years later, would go down in soccer history as the man who missed an absolute sitter for England against Brazil in the 1970 World Cup. Football's amazing. In 10 years playing for West Brom he hit 174 goals in 361 appearances and scored the winning goal when Albion won the FA Cup in 1968. That's a fantastic record by any standards. Yet if you mention his name today, the only thing people remember about him is that awful clanger in Mexico.

Well, the Baggies got off to a flying start when Clark scored in the seventh minute. Not long afterwards, I thought I had equalised with a spectacular overhead kick but the referee disallowed it for offside. Then in the 36th minute, Clark beat our offside trap for his second.

Peter Springett, our goalkeeper, kept us in the game when he pulled off a blinding save from Astle towards the end of the first half. Until then, it had been a pretty even game, but we had made two dreadful mistakes and were punished for them. We were 2–0 down at half-time and our nocturnal activities of just over 12 hours earlier seemed to be badly backfiring on us.

Before the game had kicked off, Clark had told our right winger Mark Lazarus that West Brom were on a £200 win bonus, which must have been one of the largest for a British domestic final then. When we came out for the second 45 minutes, Clive was a bit cocky and shouted over to Mark that he had already spent it. Lazarus told him that Jim Gregory had just offered Rangers £500 a man to win the game. It wasn't true, of course, but Clark's jaw hit the floor.

It's fair to say that Albion had the upper hand until there was half an hour to go. That's when the true spirit of Rangers shone through. First, Roger Morgan, our left winger, converted a Les Allen free kick with a header in the 63rd minute. Then in the 75th minute, I scored what some people have said was the defining goal of my career.

Just inside the Albion half I instantly controlled a great pass from Mike Keen. On the slippery Wembley pitch, I went from right to left as Albion's markers just seemed to float away in slow motion. Approaching Albion's box, I was looking up to pass but suddenly decided to go it alone because I knew I had to do something to save the game. Finally, about 25 yards out, I struck a right-foot shot that fizzed past Dick Shepherd and spun into the goal off the inside of a post. After that, there was no way we were going to lose.

I've heard it said that it was lucky the ball went in off the woodwork and not out, so let me tell you a little story. When I was a kid, I used to practise with a ping pong ball or an old tennis ball in the living room of our flat. I turned a chair around so the back faced me and imagined it was a goal. I played for hours just striking the ball off the legs of the chair and into the opening. The moment the ball left my foot and squeezed past the goalkeeper, I knew exactly what it would do. In fact, I didn't even see it hit the back of the net; I was already wheeling away in celebration.

The elation of bringing Rangers back from the brink of defeat was phenomenal. I could hear the whole stadium reverberating with 'Rod-nee, Rod-nee'. It was that truly incredible feeling that I shall remember for the rest of my life.

Mark Lazarus hit the winner. Ronnie Hunt played a one-two with Mark who overhit the return. In an effort to get to the ball first, Ron bulldozed his way into the penalty area as Shepherd rushed out to avert the danger. Both players were fully committed and Ron, unfortunately, caught Dick full in the chest with his studs. We all thought Hunt would be sent off there and then, it looked such a terrible foul, but the referee waved play on. When the ball bounced back out after the collision, all Mark had to do was side foot it into an open goal. Nobody could believe it when the ref gave it, but once he had, he couldn't change his mind. It was a horrible decision.

The goal stood, though, and when the final whistle went the outburst of emotion from the Rangers players was uncontrollable. It was the perfect culmination to a season in which everything had gone my way. What a moment! It was hours before I could take it all in. I just sat on the pitch and sobbed.

One moment I'll treasure forever came at the celebration dinner later that night when I discovered that Bobby Keetch had that morning placed a £500 bet on a West Brom win. Because of our party the night before, Keetchy had thought there was no conceivable way that a Third Division team could beat one from the First Division. He later told me how happy he was to lose.

As well as the League Cup, we also won the Third Division championship scoring an incredible 103 goals, just eight short of Rangers' own record for the division set in 1962.

The following week, we played Bournemouth in a league game at Loftus Road. It probably wasn't the best game I've played in, but it was certainly the game in which I played my best. I could have done anything that night. I didn't put a foot wrong. There were things I did against Bournemouth that couldn't be replicated. It was out of this world stuff. Late in the game, just inside the Bournemouth penalty box, I dragged the ball back twice from a defender. Then, as he tried to block a shot, I drove the ball through his legs on purpose with my right foot. It took off like a rocket, hit the inside of the far post and came screaming directly back to me. I controlled it with my other foot in a single touch and the ground erupted with applause. That night I scored two and made two and I don't think it was a performance that Pele or Besty could have bettered.

Sitting in the stands watching was Tottenham boss Bill Nicholson, one of the greatest judges of talent in the game. In the early sixties, Nicholson had built a fantastic double-winning side with some of the finest players seen on these shores – Jimmy Greaves, Danny Blanchflower, Dave Mackay and John White among them. He was used to seeing class. After the game, Bill went on record saying that my display had been the greatest individual performance he had seen by any player anywhere in the world. Any player, bar none, he said. In fact, the legendary Alfredo Di Stefano offered similar praise later in my career.

Bill put his money where his mouth was and offered a staggering £180,000 record cash bid a few days later to take both me and Roger Morgan to White Hart Lane. That may not sound much for two players so let me put it into perspective. At the beginning of the decade, Spurs had paid just under £100,000 to bring back Greaves from Italy. That record was broken in 1962 when Manchester United paid Torino £116,000 for Denis Law. Four years later, Alan Ball moved from Blackpool to Everton for £111,000 after pocketing a World Cup winner's medal the month before. These are some of the biggest icons in British football, so Tottenham's offer for two Third Division players was huge by any standards. Jim Gregory turned it down.

That year I had scored 44 goals in all competitions, a record which has only been surpassed by Clive Allen, Les Allen's son, who also went on to become a prolific striker with Spurs. In the 1986–87 season, he hit 12 League Cup goals to break another record of mine.

Of my 1966–67 goal haul, at least 20 were created by Les. He was a fantastic footballer, one of the most underrated players I ever came across. He had an intelligent footballing brain, and was very similar to Teddy Sheringham. He knew precisely when to pass the ball and when to hold it. The way Les weighted the ball was superb. Everybody seems to think I was the star of that Rangers team, but it's not true, not the way I see it. Les was – no doubt about it. Rangers would have won nothing without him. He was the player who made everything work. Our combination up front for Rangers was extra special and I don't think I ever played alongside a better target man. When I see Clive, which I do regularly these days, I always remind him how good his dad was.

The following season was sensational, too. At the end of 1968 we were promoted to the First Division for the first time in Rangers' history. We had been playing terrific football. Our attacks were sometimes nothing short of breathtaking. Roger Morgan and Mark Lazarus on the wings were terrifying the lives out of full-backs and dumping them on their backsides more times than I care to remember. We still had fundamentally the same team although a couple of smashing kids had broken through. One was Mick Leach, who sadly died when he was 41; and Keetchy had at last become a regular.

To get promotion, we had to beat Aston Villa in our last game at Villa Park. It was another very emotional day, and night, thanks to a Ray Bradley own goal. Late in the game, I was just about to latch on to a cross but Ray nipped in front of me and turned the ball into his own net to give us a 2–1 result.

Ipswich topped the Second Division and we went up as runners-up, edging out Blackpool on goal difference. We had gone from the Third Division to the First Division in two short years, and our home gates had rocketed to almost 22,000. In another twist, Rangers took Fulham's place in the First Division after they had finished bottom, conceding 98 goals on the way.

Any professional footballer will tell you about the zone, when you know you are going to win. It's difficult to explain. It's almost *déjà-vu*. During those couple of years, I did things with a football that a lot of people didn't think were possible. Before you even put your boots on, you know you're going to play well. You know everything's going to go right and you're going to win.

At the end of the season, Alec Stock was approached by a newspaper for an interview. He was asked about how he had come to sign me from Fulham, and how successful I had been. Alec talked about the esteem he held me in as a footballer, which was nice. We always had tremendous respect for each other. He mentioned that it was a little known fact that I had a love of art and that he believed that being artistic off the pitch contributed to how I played on it. The paper asked if I would do a portrait of Alec and they took photos of us while I sketched him. I never thought much of it but when other people saw the pictures they seemed to think it was quite odd. I suppose you can't imagine Neil Ruddock sitting down one afternoon to paint Harry Redknapp!

Before we kicked off in the top flight, Jim Gregory called me into his office one afternoon and said it was about time he looked after me. I asked how much did he want to look after me but Jim told me that he wasn't prepared to break Rangers' pay structure. He offered me a share option on 500 shares that he reckoned would do well in the next year, but I had to cough up 50 quid to exercise that option. He couldn't understand why I wouldn't accept it and told me I was turning down a lot of money. He said, 'It's not a gamble, son. It's guaranteed.'

I wasn't having any of it and stood my ground for a new contract. Backwards and forwards we went for over an hour and still I wouldn't give in. Eventually, Jim held his hands up in what I took to be a gesture of defeat. No chance. He leaned forward and told me, 'It's that or nothing.'

'OK, it's nothing,' I said, and I played the whole season on my original contract.

Less than a year later, he called me into his office, handed me an envelope and said, 'Oh by the way, Rod, I've sold those shares of yours. Here take this.'

Inside was a cheque for 10 times what the shares had been worth when he had originally offered them to me. I was amazed. I don't know why I doubted him in the first place. It was enough for a hefty deposit on the first house Jean and I bought in Epsom, near the racecourse. Jim Gregory was always as good as his word.

A lot of people may have got a different impression of him but for me he was a top man. I was so grateful to him for rescuing my career that I gave him my first England cap. Jim Gregory was quality.

We moved to Epsom because we liked the area, nothing to do with horse racing. When I read about the racing enterprises of Mick Channon and Mick Quinn, it makes me laugh. I must have been the only footballer who never had a punt. We had a neighbour on the Downs who was a trainer. One afternoon I was in the garden and he leant over the fence and said, 'Rodney, we have a stable horse going in a race on Saturday.'

'What's that?' I said. I didn't have a clue.

He said that a couple of times a year they would run one of their horses at a track where they knew it would win so everybody could make a nice few quid. He told me the name of the horse and apologised because he thought it would be only 7–2.

'Just keep it to yourself,' he added. 'It's just for us.'

I didn't have a bet and thought no more about it until he knocked on my door the following Sunday morning.

'Five to one,' he said. 'What do you think, Rod?'

I said great, terrific. Then he stood looking weirdly at me for a minute or so until I closed the door. I couldn't work it out. I thought he was a bit barmy. The next time I saw him he completely blanked me. Only later did it dawn on me that he'd come for his backhander.

What goes up can also come crashing down as we found to our cost in the 1968–69 season. I had broken my foot in pre-season training and missed the best part of the first half of the year. Before the season started, Alec Stock had resigned and was replaced in a caretaker capacity by Bill Dodgin. Contrary to what a lot of people think, Alec never picked a First Division side.

Alec was shrewd and a good judge of a situation. The year before he quit, the press had been going mad for me to play for England. I was on the back pages almost every day. One day, a Sunday tabloid phoned me. They said they wanted to do an exclusive article with me for the next Sunday, and they wanted the headline to read: 'I'm Ready For England by Rodney Marsh'. When they told me they were prepared to pay me £2,000 to do it, I almost hit the floor. Two grand was a lot of money. You could have bought a Mercedes or a BMW with it then. The reporter said, 'All the media want it and the fans would love it. We all know you think you are good enough. But are you ready to say it?'

In most players' contracts there is a clause that says you must have the club's permission to do interviews like that; so I told the newspaper I had to ask the boss first. When I saw Alec, he begged me not to do it.

'Alf Ramsey will never pick you if you do that. He doesn't like guys who blow their own trumpet,' he said. 'I know it's a lot of money but it's not worth it, son. Just go on playing as you are. Keep scoring goals and he'll look at you. He won't be able to avoid you. Banging your own drum in the papers will only ensure you won't get a chance.'

So I turned the newspaper offer down. The next Sunday morning, Jean brought the papers up to me in bed and I couldn't believe it. Splashed right across the back page was: 'Rodney's Ready For England by Alec Stock'. And he got the two thousand quid! I was really pissed off with him at first, but in the end I had to laugh.

I was sorry to see him go. Alec was almost part of my family. In 1968 when Jean went into labour with Joanna, it was Alec who took her to hospital. I couldn't drive because of a broken bone in my foot. Two years later I had a similar injury and again I couldn't take Jean to hospital to have Jonathan. This time Alec's wife Marjorie did the honours.

Rangers first game in the top division was at home to Leicester City, who we had so memorably beaten on our way to winning the League Cup 18 months earlier. This time we could only manage a draw with Les Allen coming on as substitute to score QPR's first goal at the top.

A victory over Ipswich a few weeks later was our first win and we got another not long after to reach 19th place, our highest position that year. Although we could still score goals, even without me, we couldn't stop conceding them. Things really started to go sour when we sold Roger Morgan to Tottenham for £110,000. On top of that, there was a 5–0 walloping by Coventry and an 8–1 mauling by Manchester United in Rangers' first-ever match at Old Trafford.

Before that game, Bill Dodgin gave a memorable team-talk. He told our young full-back Tony Hazell that it was his job to mark George Best. Tony didn't agree. He argued, and he could argue for England could Tony, that the best person to stop George was Bobby Keetch. Keetchy wasn't having any of it either, and insisted that he would be drawn out of his central defensive position if he tried it. On and on it went with nobody wanting to pick up Besty. You couldn't blame them for that. Better man-markers than any of our defenders had nightmares thinking about tackling George in those days. Why should we be any different?

Finally, Bill said it would be the job of the closest person to George to mark him and off we trotted for the first half. At half-time, after George had ripped us apart, the dressing-room was silent when the boss walked in.

'Er, Boss,' said Keetchy. 'That was a great plan of yours to stop Besty. Wish I'd thought of it!'

At the beginning of November, Bill Dodgin left to join Fulham and Jim Gregory appointed Tommy Docherty. What a disaster he turned out to be! The Doc was there for 28 days and if my memory serves me right we lost every game. His attitude was terrible, awful. To the players, it looked as if he had taken the job as a stopgap.

The only good thing that Docherty left behind at Loftus Road after he was sacked was a famous story. Just before he got the boot, Jim Gregory called Tommy in and told him that changes had to be made. Docherty told Gregory not to be stupid. 'You can't chuck it in now, Jim. We need you!' Gregory was not amused and Docherty was out by the end of the day.

By the time I was fit, it was too late to stop the rot. The damage had already been done. I did score on my first game back, against Nottingham Forest, but we still lost and that was the story of the rest of the season.

The only other moment of significance was at the end of

March when a 16 year old called Gerry Francis came on as a substitute for his debut. Gerry was very quiet in those days. In fact, I can't remember him saying a word in the dressing-room. I thought Gerry was a super player with terrific skills. I've frequently said so. Over the years, I have had nothing but praise for him, which is why I've been puzzled by some of the derogatory things he has said in print about me.

In spite of the losses, we still found time for fun. Near the end of our home game against Leeds, I was brought down in their box by Paul Madeley. It was a definite penalty. I took spot kicks but Paul had caught my Achilles tendon. The injury flared up straightaway making it impossible for me to take the kick. I couldn't even put my foot to the ground. So up stepped Bobby Keetch to take the penalty. He made a right hash of it, and as soon as the ball was in play, Leeds nipped down the other end and scored the winner.

After a game we used to have a drink in the players' lounge before going on to the directors' bar. The Saturday Leeds beat us, at about 10.00 p.m., a couple of us stumbled in to find Jim Gregory and his vice-chairman, Frank Voight, having a heated argument. Anybody can miss a penalty, Jim was insisting; Rod was hurt and Bob had the bottle to stand up but was unlucky. It could happen to anybody. Frank wasn't having any of it. In those situations you've got to take your chances, he roared. If not, Rangers were for the chop.

Eventually, Jim said, 'Frank, I bet you five hundred quid you can't beat me from a penalty.' Without hesitation, Frank said he was up for it.

'Any time, any place, mate,' he insisted.

Instantly, Jim ordered Alex Farmer, the groundsman, to turn the Loftus Road floodlights on, and Gregory and Voight, in their suits and ties and worse for wear, marched out on to the pitch for the shoot-out. You should have seen it.

Everyone followed them on to the pitch, drinks in hand. Jim

lined up in one of the goals and Frank placed a ball on the penalty spot. After an enormous run-up, Frank smashed the ball towards the left-hand side of the goal. Jim gave a perfect impersonation of Gordon Banks at his best, diving full length across the goalmouth and blocking Frank's piledriver. Then they both marched back into the lounge completely covered in mud and hysterical with laughter where Frank duly handed over the 500 quid.

We were back in the Second Division the following season and I suppose I could have gone to Jim Gregory and asked for a move, but I didn't. Aston Villa had been asking, along with Newcastle, Wolves and Tottenham again. I wasn't on top money at the time and I could have pushed it. Somehow, though, I didn't feel it was right. I could have earned more money elsewhere, but I've always taken other things into account. Let's just call it loyalty. As I saw it, Jim had rescued my career in the first place. I owed him. I had given my word that I would stay and I was prepared to keep it. I guess that's something else I got from my upbringing. Everyone thinks of East Londoners as Jack the lad types and maybe we are at times. But a true Cockney knows the meaning of loyalty.

Before our first game, Jim asked me how I thought the team could be improved. I told him we needed more leaders, guys who could take responsibility. If it was me, I said, I'd ask Tottenham for Terry Venables. Terry had been getting a lot of stick from the White Hart Lane crowd at the time and I reckoned he would be perfect for us.

And that's precisely what happened. Jim Gregory paid Spurs £70,000, a record transfer fee for Rangers at the time, to bring Terry to Loftus Road. And that, as Humphrey Bogart once famously said, was the start of a beautiful relationship.

It was also the beginning of the infamous West London 'Rat Pack' gatherings. The original personnel were Terry and his old Chelsea buddies Barry Bridges, who had joined us from Birmingham, and Allan Harris; plus me, of course, and Mike

Sanderson. Over the years the line-up changed but you can bet it always included Tel and yours truly. Our team-mates reckoned we were more like the Osmond Brothers!

Frank Sinatra, Dean Martin, Sammy Davis Jr, Peter Lawford and Joey Bishop cut some capers in their classic 'Rat Pack' film as they drank, gambled and partied their way through Las Vegas and Palm Springs. There were times when we weren't that far behind them as we got up to various antics right from our Ruislip training ground and into London's West End. The locations may not have the same ring, but I'm glad our scenes weren't captured on celluloid.

The Rangers Rat Packers were always together, and even then Terry was the boss, the leader. We'd meet for breakfast before training, and after training we would sometimes go drinking, frequently not returning home until two the following morning. In those days we were young and fit enough to train off the excesses.

It took a couple of years for Tel's influence to permeate the club, but right away I knew that his signing was one of the best bits of business Jim Gregory did for Rangers.

At the same time, Clive Clark came back from West Brom and Vic Mobley came in from Sheffield Wednesday to strengthen our leaky defence. I was sorry to see dear old Bobby Keetch pack his bags for the South African side Durban City. I was going to miss him for a few years although we always stayed in touch.

We had a new boss, too. Les Allen quit playing to try his luck on the manager's merry-go-round. I've said before what a great player I thought Les was but I always felt he didn't have that extra indefinable something to make it as a manager. Really, he was too nice a man and, in my opinion, not ruthless enough for a job like that. It's hard for someone to be the manager of a side that he has played for. Not many have had success. The notable exception is Kenny Dalglish but it was different when he took over at Anfield because he had the famous Boot Room to protect him.

We finished ninth in the Second Division in 1969–70. However, we did reach the last eight of the FA Cup after beating Brian Clough's rampant Derby County at home, thanks to a Dave Mackay own goal. The result equalled Rangers' best ever showing in that competition at the time. It also showed that we could still turn it on. But we couldn't cope with Chelsea in the quarter-finals. A Peter Osgood hat-trick saw to that. They went on to win the Cup.

The following year, Les had a big clear-out of players but it didn't help him to keep his job. In the January of 1971, Les was replaced by Gordon Jago.

Despite Rangers' mediocre form that season, I was still attracting a lot of attention and again finished as Rangers' top scorer. My 23 goals ensured that we at least had a mid-table place. But guess who was the second top marksman that year – Terry Venables, of course. He'd not only nicked my job as captain but also as penalty taker to boost his tally to 11. I was very happy for Terry to take over the captaincy. Even then, you could tell he was a natural.

Before the beginning of the 1971–72 season, I signed a new contract. When Jim Gregory called me in to put pen to paper, he told me if Rangers didn't get promotion that year he'd let me speak with First Division teams. I'd been playing great and he knew a load of clubs would be in for me. Also, I was 26, and that's a very important age for any footballer.

'Rod,' he said, 'I can't hold you back any longer. You've been a smashing servant for Rangers and I want to repay your loyalty.'

So we stood up and shook hands on the deal. Jim was a very tough man yet when I looked into his eyes they were misty.

In November, I at last made my England debut at Wembley,

coming on as a substitute for Francis Lee. What an experience! Although we could only manage a 1–1 draw with Switzerland, no player forgets a moment like that. And being a Second Division player in an England side full of First Division stars makes you think a bit.

The following March, Rangers were in the promotion hunt when Manchester City came in with a massive £200,000 bid. I suppose Jim Gregory could have insisted that I stayed but he didn't. Rangers missed out on going up by just a few points. City's offer was fantastic and Jim immediately told me about it.

'Do you want to go?' he asked.

'Is the Pope a Catholic?' I replied.

Coached by Malcolm Allison, Manchester City were then a world-class side, threatening to run away with the First Division title. The season Rangers had been promoted to the First Division, City had become league champions, eclipsing even the great Manchester United side in the year they won the European Cup. City had lifted the FA Cup, the League Cup and the European Cup-Winners' Cup all in about four or five years. At the time they were flying. Colin Bell, Mike Summerbee and Francis Lee were bombing teams everywhere.

The fee was massive. Only a few other British players had been sold for more. The record at the time was Alan Ball's £220,000 transfer from Everton to Arsenal.

I discussed the move with Jean and she was marvellous, right behind me, as always. We both thought the move would be right for our family. Of course, the 10 per cent signing-on fee was a big bonus but it had no bearing on the matter. I wanted to play at the highest level and Manchester City were top of the tree.

The day after City's bid, I was in a car roaring up the motorway to Manchester. Before the ink had dried on the contract I was dreaming of the trophies I would be collecting with all those fabulous players that Allison, surely the greatest coach in the game at the time, had assembled at Maine Road. If you had told me that, apart from my England caps, what I had already won was all I was destined to win in British football, I would have thought you were mad – completely mad.

CHAPTER 4

players only love you . . .

Thunder only happens when it's raining
Players only love you when they're playing

'Dreams', Stevie Nicks, Fleetwood Mac

Right, no beating about the bush, I have to hold my hands up –
I cost Manchester City the 1972 league championship. It's what
a lot of supporters have been saying for the last 25 years and it's
true. When I went there, City were five points clear at the top
of the First Division and cruising. It was down to me that we
blew it.

The transfer was a massive deal that catapulted me into the
national spotlight, but my time there was a bittersweet experience and, in retrospect, I can say it was a mistake not only for
Manchester City Football Club, but for me. Even though the
supporters during my four-year spell at Maine Road were
absolutely brilliant to me, I always felt that I had let them and
my team-mates down. I know in my heart that if Manchester
City hadn't signed me, they would have gone on to win the
championship in 1972, and I have never really come to terms
with that.

It was my fault and I take full responsibility, but let me
explain. Joe Mercer was the manager and Malcolm was the
coach. I don't think Joe wanted me but Malcolm got his way, as

he generally did then. Years later, I learned they had had a big falling out about signing me.

When I joined Manchester City, they were so superior to any other First Division side that some bookmakers made them odds-on to win the title. City had so much panache, so much style and vibrancy.

They had a playing system that was unique at the time. It was very much a rotation system although it was different from the ones used by Manchester United, Arsenal, Liverpool and Chelsea today. In the late sixties and early seventies, City played with two conventional half-backs. Mike Doyle was on the right and Alan Oakes was on the left with Tony Book, Tommy Booth and Willie Donachie behind them as defenders. When Doyle or Oakes were not needed in defence, one of them moved forward as an additional midfield player and the other stayed back. Both were more than skilful enough to do either task comfortably. It was a great system. Up front were Wyn Davies, Francis Lee, Colin Bell and Mike Summerbee with Tony Towers on the left-hand side.

When I came into the team, it completely upset the balance and while we were still playing brilliant football, we couldn't dig out the wins that we needed. That allowed Derby, Leeds and Liverpool into the chase.

For City, I played the same way as I had for Rangers, as a free spirit if you like, and that's what the team wasn't used to. It wasn't that I was playing badly. It was just that the other lads weren't used to my style and I confused them. But I was a footballer, plain and simple, not the manager. I didn't pick the team. That wasn't down to me. Sure, I had my opinions and I wasn't shy about voicing them. Yet the fact remains that it was me on the pitch and it was me who mucked up a smooth-running football machine. If I hadn't been in the side, City would have won the title, no two ways about it. So from that point of view, it was my responsibility.

First I took Wyn's place when we used a 4-4-2 formation. Then we played 4-2-4 with Davies, Summerbee, Franny Lee and me up front. But we didn't seem able to settle and the championship race turned into one of the most extraordinary finishes ever – Derby won the title when they were boozing in a bar in Majorca.

Brian Clough's side finished their league programme with a 1–0 win over Liverpool, which left them top with 58 points. One point behind were City, Liverpool and Leeds. We had also finished our games but Liverpool and Leeds both had one game to play that gave each a chance of the championship. Liverpool needed to win at Arsenal, but Leeds needed a draw only at Wolves. That would complete the double for them as they had just won the FA Cup. It looked like a formality for Don Revie's side. Yet, not for the first time, Leeds lost their bottle and the game 2–1 amid farcical allegations that some of the Wolves players had been bribed.

When the Gunners held Liverpool to a goalless draw, the Derby players were in a Calla Millor hotel restaurant having a booze up. Peter Taylor, Clough's number two, had taken them there a few days earlier. Contrary to popular belief, Cloughie wasn't even in Spain. He had taken his family and parents for a holiday on the Scilly Isles. And the two players whom I believe were responsible for Derby's success that season didn't even have a drink that night. Roy McFarland and Colin Todd celebrated with a cup of tea in a London hotel, preparing for an England game.

What really rubbed salt into City's wounds, and mine in particular, was that we had beaten Derby 2–0 a couple of weeks before in a magnificent game at Maine Road – played them off the park in fact. I scored one goal and set up the other.

Malcolm really bought me to be City's rival to George Best, even though United weren't playing wonderfully well at the time. Bobby Charlton and many of their stars were in the twilight of their careers, but there was still that extra something about them that Malcolm thought City lacked and I could provide – an extra bit of zip or fizz. Malcolm wanted me to entertain. That's what the punters pay to see. I was meant to be the icing on the cake and in that respect I don't think I let anybody down. The season before I went there, the average home gate was 31,000. For my home debut we got 55,000.

It was great because I was on an attendance bonus of £100 for every thousand spectators over the last season's average. So were all the other players. I distinctly remember Mike Doyle coming to me after the game rubbing his hands with glee at the thought of all the extra beer vouchers that would soon be in his back pocket.

'Rodney,' he said. 'You'll do for me, pal!'

Sadly, he and I were not to get on, and the word 'prat' doesn't begin to describe my feelings about Mike Doyle. If I never see him again it will be too soon.

The Maine Road fans were magnificent to me. At Rangers the fans had a chant of 'Rod-nee, Rod-nee'. City supporters adopted a top 20 hit of that year – 'Son Of My Father' by Chicory Tip – and they'd sing, 'Oh, Rodney, Rodney'. It was great. When I think of it today it gives me goosebumps.

Anyway, here's another of life's never-ending ironies. I was less than two months into being City's answer to Best, when George suddenly upped and did his first runner. Besty had been selected to play for Northern Ireland against Scotland at Hampden just after the season had finished, but instead he flew off to Spain from where he announced his retirement.

That season George had hit 18 goals in 40 league games but at the end he said that he was a mental and physical wreck. His drinking was no secret. God knows how many he would have scored if he had been sober; or, more to the point, if someone at Old Trafford had grasped the nettle and brought in some young blood to help him.

There were some great people at City, one of whom was Francis Lee. Franny, a true Lancashire lad, had joined Bolton straight from school, but when he reached his early twenties he thought the Burnden Park club's ambitions didn't match his own. He threatened to quit the game completely to concentrate on his business affairs, which caused a bit of a storm at the time. What a loss it would have been if he hadn't been allowed to move to City because Lee was one of the real stars of the late sixties and seventies. It's hard to believe now that a meagre £60,000 transfer in 1967 kept him in the game. I mean, Spurs had offered almost double that for me the same year.

I'd met Franny once previously, when I had come on as a sub for him in my first England international against Switzerland and we'd shaken hands. We hadn't really spoken. But as soon as I got to Maine Road, Francis was fantastic. He took me for drinks, to his house for dinner and generally took me under his wing. One day he asked me to go fishing with him. He picked me up at four in the morning and we sat under our coats in the pouring rain all day, alongside a river near Bolton, just the two of us. We hardly spoke a word but throughout the day he would pass me mini bottles of whiskey to keep me warm. He is a very caring and generous man.

What you see is what you get with Franny and I always looked on him as a real man's man. There was a great example of that when we went out in Manchester one night. City had played an away game, United had been at home, and Franny asked me if I fancied a quick drink in town after the game. The team coach dropped us off and we got a taxi to a drinking club in Manchester's Piccadilly.

We got there about midnight and when we walked up to the bar there must have been about a dozen United supporters having a drink there. Of course, we were spotted straightaway. We hadn't even had a sip when they started giving us some verbal – 'Rodney's a this, Franny Lee's a that . . .' – really abusive stuff. I asked Franny what he wanted to do and he said, 'We've come here for a drink and we'll have one.' But they just got louder and more aggressive the more they drank, so I said, 'Come on, Fran. It's all gonna kick off in a minute.'

We finished our drinks and left but as we walked outside some of them followed us. One guy in particular was going completely over the top. As we got to the bottom of the steps that led from the door of the club, he looked at us and said, 'Yeah, you City players haven't got the balls.' That wound Franny up. He turned on the guy and said to him, 'OK. You can have the first one.'

With that, the guy smashed a right-hander into Franny's face, but Franny didn't budge an inch, hardly even flinched. Then he really started to lay into the guy. A couple of his mates steamed in to help but I pulled them off.

'Leave it,' I said to them. 'If they want to have a knuckle, let 'em have it.' And they did.

Franny gave the guy a real beating. There was blood everywhere. The police arrived because the club owners rang them as soon as the trouble started. They carted Franny and the thug off to the station but Franny was released early the next morning without charge. I think the police saw it for what it was – the bully deserved a hiding – but the most amazing part was that the press didn't get hold of it.

I admire Franny for the things that he stands for. He has a great sense of justice. He was also one of the best footballers I have ever played alongside. He had an electric brain, could see angles other players couldn't see and was rapier-like on the pitch. It's a scandal that he won just 27 England caps.

Willie Donachie is another with whom I got on really well at City and it's priceless how we actually became friends. Like Franny, Willie helped me out a lot when I first signed for City. We were from different worlds. He was from the Gorbals in Glasgow.

On my first day at the club, he drove me to the training ground at Wythenshawe, something he did for the next three weeks, but it was odd because although we were polite and he was very friendly towards me, we never really had a conversation. It went on like that but he seemed so friendly I didn't want to say anything. I'd make the occasional comment to him in the car, he'd nod and smile; then he'd say something to me and I'd nod and smile back and then the silence would continue. Eventually, I decided I had to say something and asked him what was wrong.

'Look Rod,' Willie said, 'I love a chat. The thing is I can't understand a single word you say. I've never heard anyone talk like you before!'

It was brilliant because with his strong Scottish accent, I hadn't understood anything he'd said either. We both roared with laughter and from that day on we have been great pals. It was the start of a very good friendship.

There were other players with whom I got on well in my early years at City. Mike Summerbee sold me six dress shirts on my first day at Maine Road. I later found out that he did that to everyone when he first met them. 'Buzzer', as he was known, owned a shirt tailoring business in the heart of Manchester, but if my shirts were anything to go by, Quasimodo must have been his model because the seams were different lengths and the buttons were in the wrong places. Tony Towers, Alan Oakes and Tommy Booth, who was an excellent centre-back, were also friends. Contrary to what some people have said, I had some good friends among my City team-mates.

Oakesy was one of the most underrated players I ever saw in my life. He got so very little credit for City's success. He was very much in the Dave Mackay mould although not quite that standard. Nonetheless, he was a superb defender and there are only a handful of players who have made more league appearances. Between 1959 and 1984, he turned out for City 565 times before going on to Chester and Port Vale for another 212 games.

One night, a few of us went to George Best's club, Slack Alice, and after we fell out of there at about one in the morning, I invited a small group back to my house for a nightcap. We set off through the lanes to Prestbury where I lived. I was in the lead in a brand-new custom-built Mini Cooper that I had just bought for Jean, and Mike Horswill, who had just arrived from Sunderland, was following behind me. In the third car was Geoff Baker, the guy who had introduced me to Besty, and bringing up the rear was Colin Burns, a Slack Alice partner of George's.

We weren't going very fast and when I looked in my rear-view mirror, Colin was bumping Geoff Baker's car from behind. Then Geoff started doing the same thing to Horswill and before long the road resembled a scene from a fairground dodgems ride. There was no way I was getting involved, not with Jean's new acquisition. So I put my foot down and pretty soon I had left them behind. An hour later, I was sitting indoors wondering where the hell they had all got to. In the end I thought they had changed their minds and gone home. Just as I was about to go to bed myself, there was a loud knock on the door. When I opened it, there stood Geoff, Mike and Colin all giggling like schoolboys. There were no cars in the driveway – they were crashed in a field not far away, completely written off after the bumping game had got out of hand. Of course, I called the police who came within 10 minutes. When they got to my house, they found three guys with large glasses of brandy in their hands feeling very lucky to be alive, so they just left.

That beautiful Mini attracted some attention. It was chocolate brown with custom coachlines and had the word 'Smile' in gold leaf down the side. I got a phone call one day, completely out of the blue, from someone called Danny Gillen, who later became a good friend. Apparently, Tony Curtis, for whom Danny was working at the time, had seen Jean driving the Mini in London and he wanted to buy the car. I turned down his offer, fantastic though it was.

As well as Colin and George, Slack Alice had a third partner, Malcolm Wagner. Once, after a game, I went to the club for a drink. Outside in the three reserved-for-management parking spaces were a Mercedes sportscar, a pure white BMW and, in between them, an old Ford Granada. When I got inside I had a chat with George.

'There are some lovely cars outside, George,' I said. 'Which one's yours? The BMW?'

'No,' he said, 'that's Colin's.'

'Well, is the Mercedes yours, then?'

'No. Mine's the Granada.'

Somehow, I always thought George got the thin end of the wedge with Slack Alice.

At City, Joe Mercer was by now spending more time upstairs as general manager and less time with the team. He had been a super player in his time, and a knowledgeable manager. He was a thorough gentleman at all times. When City went on a pre-season tour of Holland at the beginning of my first full season with them, Joe decided to come along too.

Our first game was against Ajax who had been European champions for the previous two years. By the end of the season, they had won it three times in a row. Ajax were a fantastic side. They provided the nucleus of Holland's marvellous 1974 World Cup final team. Before we kicked off against them, Malcolm gave one of his superb team-talks. He was a brilliant coach, probably the best around at the time, and never missed a trick. Colin, he said, you do this and Mike, your job is that, and so on. When Malcolm had finished, he noticed Joe standing quietly by the door and, out of respect, asked him if he would like to contribute. Joe took a step forward and gave us one of his inimitable smiles.

'Well, lads,' he said. 'It's a brand new season. We're going to go for it this year and this game today, even though it is only a friendly, is very important. But Ajax aren't all they're cracked up to be. For a start, they've only got one decent player – and that's Johann Strauss . . .'

Before he left, still smiling broadly, you could have heard a pin drop. Everyone had too much reverence for Joe to think about laughing.

Malcolm was a unique character, innovative and way ahead of his time. For instance, when I first went to Maine Road, we reported for our pre-match meal at midday on a Saturday. It was a buffet of pasta, cereal, tinned fruit, juices etc., generally a carbohydrate and sugar overload. Today, when Arsene Wenger does things like that at Highbury, he's called revolutionary. Malcolm was doing it over 30 years ago.

He was also one of the greatest spenders I have ever met in my life. If I had to make a list of people who love life and love to spend loads of money, Malcolm's name would be the first; quickly followed, I might add, by Terry Venables and Bobby Keetch.

Before I arrived at Maine Road, City had won a European fixture in France. So with spirits high, as they always were when Malcolm was around, the directors, the players and everyone else went back to the hotel to celebrate. When they got there, Malcolm started the ball rolling by ordering half a dozen bottles of champagne, which didn't last long, especially with him around. Then he ordered drinks for everybody until the party atmosphere was sizzling. Hours later, in the early hours of the morning, the headwaiter interrupted Malcolm's never-ending stream of cracks and anecdotes.

'Mr Allison. Your bill, I have to tell you – it's enormous . . .' he said.

Malcolm quickly calculated that he had spent the equivalent of £1,000. He squinted at the waiter and blew cigar smoke in his face.

'Is that all? You insult me. Don't come back until it's double that!'

About six months after I joined City, we lost a midweek

fixture against Chelsea at Stamford Bridge. Back at the team's hotel, Malcolm could see that we weren't happy and he invited Franny Lee, Mike Summerbee and me out for a drink. Malcolm was probably about 45 years old then and was considered a good-looking man. He had a fantastic physique and dressed to kill in designer clothes. I know it's an overused expression but Malcolm really was larger than life.

We started at the Playboy Club and, as usual when you were with Malcolm, it was champagne all the way – bottles and bottles we had. At about one in the morning we got a phone call from some of our team-mates asking us to join them at one of London's more sophisticated nightspots. When we got there, Malcolm made his usual entrance, ordering champagne and generally taking over the place as he always did. Suddenly, in the corner, he spotted the pianist, composer and arranger James Last who had sold a colossal 50 million albums worldwide. James Last was at his peak – the only American to have more hits in the UK than Elvis Presley. Suavely, with a glass of champagne in his hand, Malcolm pulled up a seat at his table and casually introduced himself as the Manchester City manager. He explained that he was with some of his players, out on the town after a great win, and asked would he mind playing a tune for the lads because we were all great fans.

Astonishingly, James Last agreed, made his way to the piano and started playing one of his world-famous hits. Mike Summerbee, as drunk as the rest of us, walked over to the piano and started singing 'We ain't got a barrel of money'. In an instant, Franny and I had joined in, drowning out the pianist and his number one hit. Amazingly, instead of slamming the piano lid down and storming off, James Last became our backing player. We finished with all the lads giving us a standing ovation. James Last was brilliant for joining in the fun. When he returned to join his guests, Malcolm had already sent over four bottles of champagne as a thank you.

Not long after that cameo performance, I got a knock in a Saturday home game and had to go to the Wythenshawe training ground the following morning for treatment. When I arrived, Malcolm was already there and had just finished working on the weights. Franny Lee was also having treatment.

At about midday when we had finished with the physio, Malcolm came to check on us. When he was satisfied that the injuries were responding, he invited us for lunch. We went to the Brooke House Hotel in Wilmslow Road, just around the corner from the ground. We used to call it the club hotel. The guy who owned it was called Jim Barker. I'll never forget him. He was a super man and a City fanatic. When we got to the bar, Malcolm ordered Bollinger and we spent the afternoon telling jokes and generally having a good time.

In those days, Malcolm was so easy to be with, always very upbeat. After a few more bottles of champagne we had a little party going. When it got to about two o'clock and our sixth or seventh bottle, I phoned Jean and warned her that I was going to be a bit late. Jean has always been brilliant about things like that. Not every footballer's been so lucky, believe me. I knew a lot of players who couldn't take the dog for a walk without permission from the wife.

We carried on drinking all afternoon until we had emptied a staggering 23 bottles of champagne. Finally, Malcolm surveyed the one remaining bottle from the two cases that were still on the bar and called Jim over.

'Jim,' he slurred. 'No more. I'm not going to have the twenty-fourth bottle. I don't want people to think I'm a flash bastard!'

With that he wrote out a cheque for the damage and staggered through the door. Despite the amount we had drunk, when we got outside into the hotel grounds, Franny climbed into his brand-new lime green Mercedes, his prize possession that he had collected just days before – and thankfully drove it straight into the back of a Triumph Herald. He got a taxi home instead.

Malcolm was a great coach and it was a huge surprise when, towards the end of the season, he called me into his office and said, 'Rod, I just want to let you know something and before I make a decision I would like your opinion. I've been approached by Crystal Palace to be their manager.'

I was stunned. Less than 12 months earlier, City had at last fully recognised what a brilliant football mind he had by making him the Maine Road manager. They had an outside chance of a European place next season. Why would a guy who was in charge of one of the top teams in the First Division even consider going to another that was languishing at the bottom and destined to be relegated?

But Malcolm's decision wasn't really a football one. He had been having an affair with Serena Williams, a Playboy bunny girl, and she wanted him to move down to London.

I told him, as I would tell anybody, 'You've got to do what you feel is right. Do what your heart tells you.'

I respected Malcolm for asking my opinion. How many other coaches or managers would have done that? Not many I bet. The day he left, I had a strange feeling that I was on my own – a bit of a premonition if you like. But I didn't lose touch with him. In the years to come, our paths collided as much as crossed.

Malcolm couldn't stop Palace from going down that year or struggling the next. If he had stayed at Maine Road, I feel he could have stopped City from going downhill as they did over the next couple of years.

After Malcolm left, the Maine Road managership became a bit of a merry-go-round. First Johnny Hart, who was a youth-team trainer as I remember, took over. Then there was Ron Saunders and Tony Book followed him. From the moment Hart took charge, it started to go wonky. Johnny was there for six months before ill health forced him to resign but in that time he pulled off a transfer that surprised everybody in football. He persuaded Denis Law to return to Maine Road from Old Trafford.

Ron Saunders didn't last six months. The City board had been impressed by the way he had taken Norwich to the League Cup final the year before – they had lost to Spurs 1–0 – and liked his reputation as a bit of a disciplinarian. However, it was well known to everybody in the game, except of course the Maine Road hierarchy, that Saunders wasn't the best communicator and that this had led to his downfall at Carrow Road. It wasn't a surprise to most people when he had a similar problem at City, which is probably why he was sacked five months after taking us to the 1974 League Cup final. Wolves beat us 2-1.

It was so disappointing to lose at Wembley. As someone who has a win-at-all-costs mentality, that defeat made me so mad I chucked away my loser's medal as I walked off the pitch. A few weeks later when I had calmed down, I wrote to the FA asking for a replica but all I got was a curt reply saying no. I should have known better really. Lancaster Gate doesn't know much about football so why should I have expected them to appreciate emotion? (By the way, if anyone out there has it, any chance I can have it back?)

Although we lost at Wembley, City supporters did at least have something to celebrate. Not long before the season ended, our game against Manchester United at Old Trafford turned into one of the most heated derby battles the city has ever seen and a riot towards the end forced the match to be abandoned.

To avoid relegation, United had to win and one of their relegation rivals, Birmingham or West Ham, had to lose. With eight minutes to go, Denis Law cheekily back-heeled the ball into the United net right in front of the fans who had once idolised him. It looked like he had condemned his former club to the Second Division.

At the time, I had gone off with an injury and was sitting on the bench but I could clearly see that Denis's face was ashen. He looked like he had seen a ghost. He didn't seem to know where he was and was wandering around in a confused state. I said to Tony Book, who was sitting next to me, 'Get him off, Skip. He's gone.'

Before we could get to him, hundreds of hooligans rushed on to the pitch to try to stop the game and force a replay. During the following chaos, the ref ordered us off. As it turned out, it wouldn't have made any difference if United had beaten us because both Birmingham and West Ham won their games.

In the dressing-room afterwards, Denis was as miserable as I've seen him. His goal hadn't relegated United but he later told me that only one other game had made him feel as bad and that was England winning the World Cup!

The really depressing event of that season was the disgraceful manner in which the FA sacked England manager Sir Alf Ramsey, seven years after he had made England the world champions. The greatest football manager in the history of English football, the man who gave us all a moment to feel proud, wasn't even given the chance to resign. I don't think Alf ever recovered from the way it was done and for sure English football hasn't. The decision disgusted most professionals at the time. In fact, it still does.

After Ron Saunders went, City appointed Tony Book as manager and I took over as captain. Before the 1974–75 season kicked off, Book made the first of many cock-ups by selling Franny Lee to Derby for £110,000. In doing so, Book didn't just shoot himself in the foot, he almost blew City's legs off.

'Lee One Pen', as he was affectionately known by the press because of the number of penalties he was awarded through his bravery in the box, went on to collect a second championship medal at the Baseball Ground before retiring aged 32 the following year.

The really comical thing about the transfer was that Book signed Barney Daniels from non-league Telford as Franny's replacement. I just shook my head when I heard because that was when I knew Manchester City were about to turn a silk purse into a sow's ear.

Barney was a smashing lad but even he would admit he was no substitute for Franny. One of the first things Tony Book did was tell Barney to take all the free kicks. I think he must have seen him hit a one-in-a-million shot on target during training because he was hopeless. Previously, the job had been mine and Colin Bell's, much like Beckham and Giggs at Manchester United today. I was very much in the David Beckham mould at free kicks. Barney could strike a ball all right. In fact, he had more power than almost any other player around. His problem was that he had absolutely no clue where the ball was going. In one game, I think we ran out of balls because he'd lamped so many out of the ground.

However much I watched Barney, I could never understand what it was that had made Tony Book buy him in the first place. A few months later it dawned on me. Although Tony had been a terrific player – one of the most underrated defenders around at the time – as a manager he sometimes lacked judgement. I thought his coach, Ian McFarlane, was worse. Unfortunately, I couldn't cover up how I felt about them.

I was a bit of a rebel I suppose, and I would go out of my way to test Book's resolve. Even though I was captain, I was still very anti-establishment. For example, the club had a rule about wearing a jacket and tie to all away matches, and on two occasions I turned up in an open-necked shirt. Tony warned me on both occasions that the next time he would fine me two weeks' wages. Sure enough, at our next away match, against Chelsea, the night before the game Book said to the whole team that anyone not wearing a tie the next day would be fined. I knew he had said it for my benefit. Thinking about how I was then makes me wonder how Alex Ferguson handled a player like Eric Cantona – better than Tony Book handled me it would seem.

Somewhat half-heartedly I began trying to find a tie – I asked my room-mate Willie Donachie but he had just one tie with him, and that was as hard as I tried. I didn't really want to find a tie anyway. The following morning I went down for the team breakfast and, according to the rules, I did have a tie on – of sorts. I went downstairs with the electric cord from the kettle in our room fastened around my neck, with the plug stuffed in my inside pocket. When Tony saw it, I told him it was a new American fashion. Even though he must have been fuming, he had to concede to my creativity. It was funny but I regret doing it because that was the beginning of the end of our working relationship.

It didn't help when I bought a sweatshirt in Manchester with a logo emblazoned on the front saying 'Smile'. Even though I hadn't meant it as a dig at him, Tony took it personally! Two days later he came in to the ground wearing a T-shirt emblazoned with the word 'Play'. Clever, I thought, but an overreaction on his part. However, looking back it was inevitable, after everything I put him through, that our relationship would not work.

In 1974, a bombshell hit the game when Bill Shankly announced his retirement at the age of 58. It was totally unexpected. He had taken over at Anfield at the end of 1959 when Liverpool were a Second Division side. Two and a half years later, the Reds were in the top flight. Shankly guided them to three league championships, two FA Cups and a UEFA Cup with three outstanding sides. He was one of the game's legends. When I played in his testimonial the following year, he gave me one of the biggest compliments that I have ever had when he told me that he had made a bid for me when I was an 18 year old at Fulham. Many people think of me as a showy player who put entertaining the fans above the interests of the team, but if that were the case, why did Shankly, who it was well known didn't tolerate slackers, try to take me to Anfield? He told me that Fulham turned his offer down but I didn't know anything about the bid at the time.

Just before I was lining up to go out for a Don Revie XI against Liverpool for his benefit, he took me to one side.

'Rodney,' he said. 'I've always thought you were great. I wish I could have had you at Anfield. Those tricks of yours, I love them. There's nobody in the game who can do them like you. Listen. I want you to do a few tonight. Just to make it special for me.' Then, unbuttoning his jacket, he took a handkerchief from his top pocket and added, 'You see this, Rodney. Look out for me when you're out there. I'll be sitting in the directors' box. And when I wave the handkerchief, I want you to do a trick.' Then he winked and walked away.

I laughed to myself. I mean, did he honestly think I could conjure up a bit of magic to order? Then I wondered if he was taking the mickey. Bill Shankly – what an amazing man! He had the ability to make you feel 10 feet tall and yet not let you get carried away with yourself – all at the same time. No wonder he was so successful.

During half-time, the great man and some of his contemporaries played a mini five-a-side game. They had the 40,000 Kopites cheering and applauding with their non-stop effort, even though many of those playing with Shanks were in their sixties.

The break lasted almost half an hour and when I asked when we would be going on for the second half, I was told by the referee, 'Just as soon as we can get Shankly off the pitch. We've been trying for ten minutes but he says the score is 4–4 and he refuses to come off until someone's hit a winner!'

At the start of the 1975–76 season, Dennis Tueart and Joe Royle arrived at Maine Road and with them on board we played some great football at times with plenty of goals. But although we were battering sides, we weren't as consistent as we should have been and it led to some strong words from Book and McFarlane. I didn't feel it was all the players' fault. I felt the messages from the management team undermined confidence on the pitch. There didn't seem to be any direction or guidance, no plan whatsoever.

Early in the season we beat Norwich 6–1 in the League Cup; Dennis Tueart was outstanding. Then I got the winner with a diving header in a 3–2 result at Highbury. Not long after that, we found ourselves a goal down in a league game against Norwich and what I did towards the end of the game was the beginning of the end. With a few minutes left we got a free kick just outside their box and I told our big centre-half Dave Watson to go up for it. As he did, I could hear Book and McFarlane shouting for Watson to stay back. I couldn't believe it. Today you see goal-keepers going forward in situations like that. What have you got to lose?

'Fuck 'em,' I said. 'Get on up there, David.'

He scored an equaliser from the free kick with a magnificent diving header. David was always capable of doing things like that. I couldn't understand why those two twerps running the team had argued with me in the first place.

Predictably, it led to a big bust-up with Book and McFarlane in the dressing-room afterwards. I thought how dense can you two get? My decision had been proved correct and at least we had a point.

The following week we played Burnley off the park at home and ended up with a 0–0 draw. On the pitch I'd had a fun day, really enjoying myself. The points could have been in the bag but for some dodgy decisions. Afterwards Ian McFarlane made a complete clown of himself. He stood there ranting and raving, making no sense whatsoever at times. Dennis Tueart told him to calm down.

'Don't lose your rag, Ian. It's still a good point,' he said.

McFarlane launched a left-hook at Tueart, knocking him completely off his feet. That's when I was convinced everybody had lost the plot. Somehow the press found out about the punch-up between McFarlane and Tueart and the newspapers the following day were full of it. The next week the chairman, Peter Swales, called me into his office.

'Rodney,' he said. 'As captain, I want your honest opinion about Tony Book and Ian McFarlane.' So I told him.

'If you want my honest opinion, I'll give it. They're both fucking useless.'

Just after that meeting, Tony Book called me into his office.

'If you think I'm effing useless,' he said, 'it's not going to work. Do you want to take it back?'

'No chance,' I said. 'In fact, thinking about it more, you're not that good.'

And that was the end of my Manchester City career. I was immediately transfer-listed, ordered to train with the kids and injured players, and never pulled on a City shirt again.

It was a tragedy that, within weeks of me being transfer-listed, Colin Bell suffered the horrific knee injury that eventually ended his career. City lost two of their most influential players in a very short space of time.

The experience was soul destroying. One minute I was captain of Manchester City and a hero; the next I was changing with the juniors who only days before had been asking for my autograph. It was humiliating. I felt as if I was on the scrapheap. It was the lowest point of my career. I will never forget the way Tony Book treated me, and I will never forgive him either. What mucked me up psychologically was that nobody except a few close friends stood by me; that really hurt. At times like that people show their true colours. Willie Donachie, Franny Lee, Joe Royle and Asa Hartford did and are good friends to this day.

The supporters were nothing short of great. Some of them erected huge banners and signs asking why I wasn't in the team. There were even protest demonstrations outside the Maine Road stadium entrances. Years later, Peter Swales wrote in a football magazine that during the week I was booted out he got a staggering 7,000 letters from disgruntled fans begging for me to stay. Why on earth he didn't say so then, beats me.

As the weeks drifted on, I was getting lower and lower emotionally. I must have been a real pain to be around but I was confused. I couldn't understand why I was being treated in that way. Every player knows when they're past it, believe me. But before the bust-up I had been playing some of the best football of my career. I was at my peak and brimming with confidence. Book and McFarlane knocked that out of me in a few moments.

Four or five teams did come in for me – Belgian side Anderlecht, Aston Villa, Crystal Palace and Birmingham among them – but I just didn't want to go to any of them. I thought if I kept hanging on, things would turn round, but they never did.

Towards the end of the year I went to Ireland for six guest appearances for Cork Hibs. They had offered me £600 a game with the whole amount in cash up front. It was more money than they later paid Besty to turn out for them.

When the Cork chairman picked me up from the airport for the first match, I politely asked about my money. He said there was no problem and he would give it to me when we got to the ground. So after meeting the other players and going through the pleasantries, I reminded the chairman of his arrangement but nothing was forthcoming. So I refused to get changed. Ten minutes before the kick-off, the chairman came back into the dressing-room and when he saw me still sitting there in my suit he got into a bit of a panic. I had to remind him that a deal was a deal. Within minutes he had handed me a shoebox full of readies.

'There you go, Rod,' he smiled. 'Happy to oblige.'

Only when I was lining up ready to go out on the pitch with the box in my hand did it dawn on me how dumb I was. There was nowhere in the dressing-room where I could lock the money and I couldn't take it with me. Red-faced, I approached the chairman and asked him if he would mind looking after it until the game had finished. We both saw the funny side and it was the first time I'd laughed in weeks!

Back in Manchester, I was no better. I should have been able to deal with it but at the time it was easier said than done – captain of one of the biggest clubs in the country one minute, and the next I didn't exist. I suppose I had contributed to the situation by pushing things too far, testing Book and McFarlane so that they came back and completely slaughtered me in the way they did. That's not how it should be done, though. The situation could have been handled in a much better fashion.

We had an awful Christmas. In the New Year I went to have a look at things at Anderlecht and had talks with Villa, but I couldn't shake myself out of my malaise. Then I received a phone call from Ken Adam who was a football agent at the time. He had been told by fashion photographer Terry O'Neill that Elton John had heard about my Maine Road misery. Would I like to be Elton's guest for a few days in Los Angeles where he was due to give a concert at the Dodgers Stadium? I was flabbergasted. If I fancied it, said Ken, I could travel on his private plane. It transpired that Elton was negotiating to buy the Los Angeles Aztecs who played in the North American Soccer League, and he wanted to sign Besty and employ me as player-manager. I didn't need asking twice, and I'm sure Jean appreciated me out of the house just to give her a break.

So off I went with Ken and Terry in Elton's private plane to have a look at America. It was great. The second night we were there, Ken and I went out to dinner with Ray Cooper, then Elton's drummer, and I got a phone call from a T. Beauclerc Rogers IV. I thought anyone with a handle like that must be worth speaking to! Beau Rogers was the chairman of the Tampa Bay Rowdies, who were also in the NASL.

'Rodney,' he said. 'Before you sign for Los Angeles, would you come and have a look at Tampa Bay?'

'Where's Tampa Bay?' I said.

The next morning, two first-class return tickets arrived and Ken and I were off to Florida for two days. I'm glad we went because I thought Florida was great from the moment I stepped off the plane. I was so impressed that I agreed to join the Rowdies there and then.

Returning to California, we took in Elton John's superb

concert before flying back to England. I thanked Elton for thinking of me but told him of my decision to go to Florida. He gave me his blessing and wished me luck. He's a first-class guy, in my opinion. Interestingly, for reasons of his own, Elton pulled out of the deal to buy the Aztecs and bought Watford instead.

A lot of rock 'n' rollers were getting into football clubs in the States then. Peter Frampton was involved with Philadelphia Fury and the Warner Brothers record company controlled the New York Cosmos. There was even talk that Mick Jagger would buy into the Cosmos as he regularly went to their games together with Rick Wakeman. It made the US soccer scene a real media circus.

I thought going to the Rowdies would be a breath of fresh air – just what I needed. Back in Manchester, after I had announced what I was doing, it didn't take long for the backstabbers to crawl out of the woodwork. After I left City, all the people who never said things to my face suddenly couldn't wait to criticise me, including some of my old team-mates. The thing that got me most at the time was the speed with which so many seemed to change their tune. Up until the shit hit the fan, we had been playing brilliant football and there was a great atmosphere in the dressing-room. We had just come back off a 6–1 demolition of Norwich in the League Cup and we'd had a 3–2 win at Highbury against a magnificent Arsenal team. Everything had been going so well; everyone seemed happy. I was captain of the team and nobody seemed to have a problem with me. Then it seemed to be open season on Rodney Marsh.

As I have said before, I understand if people don't like me. I know I can be a bit of an arsehole, and I let very few people get close, so they judge me on what they see. But I'm man enough to take it if people say things to my face. What I hate is when it's done behind my back. Once I left, one or two people were quoted in the press slagging me off.

I was really surprised, and disappointed, that one of my critics was Joe Corrigan, the current goalkeeping coach at

Liverpool. I was hurt; it seemed Joe had a very short memory. Not long after I joined City, he asked me to stay on after training and help him work on his game and I was happy to oblige. From then on, I spent many afternoons helping him polish his technique with crosses, shots and set-pieces. I considered Joe a friend. We used to go to each other's houses and our wives were quite friendly. What Joe was quoted as saying then still rankles.

At a time when I needed support, those around me began turning the knife. I knew I had friends at the club who would always be loyal – Franny, Willie, Joe Royle and Asa – but when you are low and your self-esteem has taken a knock, it's hard to have people suddenly turn on you and start slagging you off behind your back. I'd rather face it straight on. Dennis Tueart, one of the other senior professionals at the time who is, incidentally, still on the board at Manchester City, also was quoted making some comments I did not appreciate.

A few of the City players who had played a straight bat with me organised a goodbye party in Slack Alice's, which I thought was nice of them. During my problems they hadn't wanted to get caught in the crossfire, which I could understand. Anyway, unexpectedly Dennis Tueart showed up at the private party, held out his hand and said, 'Good luck, Rod.' I couldn't believe it.

'Fuck off,' I said and I didn't speak to him again for about 20 years until he came up to me at one of the roadshows that George and I used to do and asked me how I was, as if nothing had happened.

'I still think you're a bastard,' I said, 'but I can't remember why.'

Wilf McGuinness, who was the master of ceremonies that night, almost fell over.

'You liked me as a player,' Tueart said. 'We just didn't get on socially.'

In spite of my misery at the time of my City troubles, I still kept tabs on my old Queens Park Rangers buddies. They were having the best finish to a season in their history and only just missed out on the First Division championship by a whisker to Liverpool. One point clear at the top of the table, they had an agonising 10-day wait for Liverpool to play their last game away to Wolves.

Again Molineux had a hand in seventies football history. Bob Paisley's side went in at half-time a goal down and Rangers had one hand on the trophy. But Kevin Keegan, John Toshack and Ray Kennedy were all on target in the second half, giving Liverpool their ninth league title. Wolves were relegated.

I felt for Rangers, even in my personal gloom. They must have been gutted for they had dropped just three points in their last 15 games when it was two points for a win. Nonetheless, Rangers had qualified for Europe for the first time as runners-up and were one of the most entertaining sides around.

It was my move to Manchester City that had financed the rebuilding of the team. With the money from my transfer fee they were able to buy Frank McLintock, Arsenal's 1971 double-winning captain, and Stan Bowles, whom they got from Carlisle for £110,000. Stan would have been a bargain for double that. There was enough cash left for them to buy Don Givens, a front man from Luton, and Dave Thomas, a tricky winger from Burnley. QPR were also able to hang on to the useful players they had and some terrific kids who were coming through.

What made that Rangers team tick was the special under-standing between Bowles and Francis. It was telepathic really. There have been some great double acts – Keegan and Toshack, Peter Beardsley and Gary Lineker for England and, yes, Les Allen and me on our day – but there haven't been many better than Stan and Gerry. It was no surprise to me when Don Revie made Francis the England captain and it's a real shame he had so many injury problems. Why Stan made just five international appearances is a mystery.

My parting shot before flying from England to Tampa made

all the newspapers. Before boarding the flight I said that football in England had become a grey game, played on grey days by grey people! As the plane taxied to the runway it was raining heavily. Depression is a strange animal. Before Manchester City treated me in the way they did, I'd not known what it was like. And I didn't know that it would take a few years to flush it out of my system.

CHAPTER 5

someone helped save my soccer life

Go West, young man.

Horace Greeley, *New York Tribune*
founder and editor

'Rodney Marsh is known as the white Pele,' announced the owner of the Tampa Bay Rowdies at one of my first press conferences to a mass of media broadcasters.

'No,' I told everybody. 'Pele is known as the black Rodney Marsh!'

That comment didn't endear me to some of the Tampa and New York media, but that's the way I am and always will be. Take it or leave it. I meant it as a joke, but if you don't believe in yourself, who else is going to believe in you? I wasn't going to be put into second place by anybody.

A lot of the Tampa sports reporters resented me from the very first moment they saw me. They thought I was stand-offish and conceited, and that was just a couple of the nicer things they said. But I'd been used to the British press – the all-conquering hero one minute and something that you scrape off your shoe the next.

What made me laugh about some of the Tampa guys was that after they'd had a pop at me they couldn't understand why I wouldn't talk to them after a game. Sometimes I would just shower and change, then jump into my car and drive off without saying a word. Fortunately, not all the media were hostile and I eventually became quite pally with a couple of them.

But so what if the press thought I was arrogant? The fans didn't. They loved me and the Rowdies right from the first ball I kicked in the Tampa Stadium, which to me was all that mattered. I developed a brilliant relationship with the fans and had an incredible four seasons there.

The Rowdies president and co-owner was George Strawbridge Jr, an exceptionally wealthy man from Philadelphia who also owned one of the country's top horse-racing stables and the world famous Campbell Soup empire.

T. Beauclerc Rogers IV was also from Philadelphia. He was the executive vice-president and co-owner. Beau was a typical entrepreneurial, fast-moving American businessman with the obligatory digits after his name, which might have fooled a lot of people. Beau was soccer savvy for an American and through his dynamism the Rowdies had been to the NASL finals. But they hadn't been getting great crowds, until I arrived that is. After that they just took off. Tampa had never seen anything like it before.

I signed a four-year deal with the Rowdies on 12 January 1976 and made my first appearance in a Rowdies' shirt in a six-a-side tournament with all the hype and razzmatazz that only happens in the States. Amid tons of ticker tape, I was brought into the arena on top of a 1920s fire engine, the sirens clanging and wailing, and I handed dozens of roses to girls in the crowd. It was real carnival stuff.

The season started in earnest in April and I made my debut against Chicago in a packed Tampa Stadium. At a press conference before the kick-off, Beau had said, 'If Rod puts a good act together, he'll be the pied piper of America – and he'll make himself a fortune. Entertainment is what I want, and Rodney is the man to give it. He is good-looking, has oodles of charisma and, by golly he can sure make that ball talk.' And that's precisely what I did, scoring one and making another as we blew the Illinois side off the pitch.

Lining up for the Rowdies that year were some old British stalwarts including former Chelsea and Millwall striker Derek Smethurst, West Ham's Clyde Best and Watford and Sheffield United winger Stewart Scullion. Stuart Jump and Mark Lindsay from Crystal Palace were also there. For once I was pleased to see Liverpool's Tommy Smith on my side, having felt the weight of his challenges far too often in the past.

The head coach at Tampa was Eddie Firmani. In his day, South African-born Eddie had played in both England and Italy and his £35,000 move to Sampdoria from Charlton in 1955 was a British record.

Firmani became quite a big name in North American soccer over the years and was the first man to lead an NASL team to two titles. Eddie coped very well, mentally and physically, after losing a thumb in a water-skiing accident not long after he went to Florida. Nicknamed the 'Golden Turkey', Firmani is still coaching Major League Soccer teams today, aged 68. He took charge of the New York/New Jersey MetroStars when the league was launched in 1996.

While Eddie was at Tampa, it's true to say that we had some ups and downs. After one row, he tried to off-load me back to England permanently and if it hadn't been for Beau Rogers he might have got his way.

Phil Woosnam's North American Soccer League was born in 1968, after the FIFA-sponsored United States Soccer Association and the renegade National Professional Soccer League merged. That it got off the ground at all was down to the perseverance of Lamar Hunt, a shrewd businessman who was the architect of American football's SuperBowl.

The NASL had struggled during its infancy but by the mid 1970s it was starting to roll, mainly because of superb American marketing and some massive investment. Before that, about half the League's players were home-grown and the rest were unknown imports from Europe and South America. The playing standard was equivalent to that of the Nationwide Division Three. The New York Cosmos upped the ante when, with the backing of the Warner Brothers record company, they shelled out the £3.5 million a year it took to capture Pele. Today's equivalent would be around £40 million. In fact, the NASL also stumped up some of that cash. It was a bit like the Premiership chipping in to assist United to buy Figo! But Pele's presence gave the NASL the credibility it had previously lacked. When Italian superstar Giorgio Chinaglia followed Pele from Lazio, all the other clubs just went bananas buying up every European and South American star they could lay their hands on; and suddenly players who had once turned up their noses at the thought of joining a US team were queuing up to go there. It was wild.

Besty had the opportunity to team up with Pele and Chinaglia at the Cosmos but turned it down because he preferred the more relaxed atmosphere of the West Coast with the Los Angeles Aztecs. Perhaps George thought he was recapturing his youth because when he signed for the Aztecs he was, at 30, their youngest player! Or perhaps it was the prospect of being in California with kindred spirits such as former Chelsea idol Charlie Cooke, surely one of the most talented players ever to grace the First Division. Other big names coming into the NASL were Eusebio, who went to Canadian side Toronto from Boston, Bobby Moore (San Antonio) and Geoff Hurst (Seattle).

The Cosmos were the American Manchester United and grounds up and down the East Coast were filling up, but curiously George's lot could only pull in average gates of 10,000. Other Brits with league experience included Ron Futcher, Gordon Wallace, Jim Ryan, Brian Tinnion, Phil Parkes, Bobby Clark, Geoff Barnett, Jim Cumbes and Ade Coker. Coker had hit one blinding goal for West Ham, which was shown on TV for years, before disappearing into obscurity,

My parents Lil and Bill get married in the East End in 1943, surrounded by family.

My mum and dad in Jaywick Sands, near Clacton, in the summer of 1955. This was the only holiday we ever had.

My first trip abroad with Alexander Boys Under 15s side to Holland in 1959. David Turner, Michael Brown and me pose for the camera.

Playing for Alexander Boys Under 15s in 1959.

Halcyon days: Bobby Moore, Bestie and me on the Craven Cottage pitch after arriving back from the States for the 1976–77 season with Fulham.

George and I play in one of the most entertaining games ever, the now infamous 4–1 victory over Hereford at Craven Cottage in 1976.

Really big money began to be pumped into American soccer during the first season I was there. Huge American conglomerates and Arab moguls all wanted part of the action. They weren't making any money out of it. The League never made a penny. It was just a big toy for a lot of wealthy influential people. But that's what's so great about America. It's full of people whose enthusiasm is infectious. When they get behind something, it's a wonderful experience just to be part of it. I can't stand to hear America being knocked. Constructive criticism is one thing but don't slate enthusiasm. Channel it, for heaven's sake.

Despite ruffling a few feathers early on, I went on to have a brilliant season, fantastic. That year the scoring system was six points for a win, three for a draw and a bonus point if you scored three goals. It made it all very interesting, particularly for us because Smethurst finished as top goalscorer with 20 goals and I hit 11, although Chinaglia's 11 assists put him on top of the strikers' ratings. The Cosmos may have had the most money but at the end of the year they didn't have the most points. In spite of all their talent, they had got off to a poor start under former Watford and Sheffield United coach Ken Furphy, who was soon replaced. If you can't build a side around Pele, who can you build one around?

So in the Eastern Conference, New York took second billing to us. In the division championships we gave them another beating, but in the Conference championships we missed a place in the Soccer Bowl after losing to eventual winners Toronto.

It had been an interesting experience. Pele, of course, was named player of the year and he didn't get the award on the sympathy vote, either. Firmani was the coach of the year and I got a place in the NASL's first all-star team. Even now it makes fascinating reading. Lining up 4-3-3 it was: Arnie Mausser (Tampa); Bobby Moore (San Antonio), Mike England (Seattle), Tommy Smith (Tampa), Keith Eddy (New York); Ramon Mifflin (New York), Antonio Simoes (Boston/San Jose), Rodney Marsh

(Tampa); George Best (Los Angeles), Pele (New York), Giorgio Chinaglia (New York).

Another high spot was being picked to play for Team America. For the American Bicentennial celebrations, the United States Soccer Federation organised a tournament with Brazil, Italy and England. It was intended to promote the game to American audiences at large, a mini World Cup. But instead of selecting a representative US side, which wouldn't have stood a chance, it was decided that a team comprising NASL players would compete as Team America. It was an honour for me to be chosen for the team, to be managed by Ken Furphy, along with Pele, Best, Bobby Moore and Chinaglia, but I declined.

When I dropped out, some very nasty rumours started in the press that really annoyed me. It was said that George and I walked out after Furphy refused to guarantee both of us a starting place in the line-up of all three games. That was rubbish. I declined the invitation to play because I believed, and still do, that it wasn't right for non-Americans to be selected for the team. I mean, it was their 200th birthday party, not mine.

The highlight of my first year in American soccer, though, had nothing to do with football. In spite of the violence I have always been a boxing fan. When I look back at my upbringing, the only time there wasn't any trouble was when we discussed boxing! Halfway through the season, the Rowdies had a game against the US national side in Memphis, Tennessee, and the guest of honour at the after-match dinner was none other than Muhammad Ali. The real honour was mine because I sat next to the great man throughout the meal. I'm sure everybody can name someone they admire and respect whom they never expect to meet. For me, that man was Ali.

When you are a footballer you get to meet a lot of interesting people, but being introduced to the Man was special. He wasn't into soccer, and I didn't have the chance of much personal conversation – anyway, it didn't seem appropriate – but he was wonderful company. He was charismatic and a brilliant and witty speaker. I consider that evening one of the highlights of my sporting career.

Listening to him, I distinctly remembered going to watch him train at the White City before his first fight with Henry Cooper in 1963. Along with my dad and some mates we had to wait an hour for Cassius Clay, as he was then, to come out and climb into the gymnasium training ring. It seemed like there were thousands of people milling around, all waiting with an anticipation that is quite different from football. Throngs of press were there, too. It was almost like waiting for royalty. Eventually, one of the trainers came out, without a microphone I might add, and the place was instantly silent.

'Ladies and gentlemen,' he said. 'Cassius Clay.'

When Ali came through the door, his head was covered with a bleached white towel and the whole of his body by a white robe. You couldn't see a piece of flesh at all. At first nobody was sure that it was him. I mean, it could have been a publicity stunt – which wouldn't have surprised anyone considering some of the antics that Clay was regularly getting up to in those days. Nonetheless, nobody dared to challenge the man in front of us.

He got into the ring and for several minutes danced and shadow boxed, flicking out first his right then his left arm, jabbing and moving. The co-ordination and balance were fantastic. Then he walked to one of the ring's corners and his trainer removed the robe and towel, and everybody just gasped.

I blinked. I couldn't believe it. Right in front of us was the most magnificent athlete I have ever seen. You may have watched TV clips of Ali in those days, but they don't begin to capture what it was like to see him in real life. His body would have shamed both Hercules and Adonis. He was sweating a little, just enough to give a sheen.

There is a very overused word these days, particularly in America, and that is 'awesome'. The only time I have ever dreamed of using it in all my years as a sportsman was looking at Ali that day. I knew I was fit and I'd already seen some superb athletes, but the sight of Ali then was humbling.

So to sit down and join him at dinner later in my life was fabulous. I have read a lot about him since and he remains in my mind the greatest athlete of all time.

Another high spot that year was when Malcolm Allison came to visit. One day Beau Rogers asked me what I thought of him. Beau had loads of football contacts and had been hearing some rave reviews about Malcolm's abilities, particularly from some of the ex-pats who were flooding into the American game. He asked me whether I thought it would be a good idea to bring Malcolm over for a month during the UK close season to help with the coaching. I told Beau how much I thought of Malcolm and Eddie Firmani agreed.

So Malcolm came over and stayed with me in the apartment I had at the time overlooking Tampa Bay. After just a few days with the team, his silky charm had already begun to woo everybody, including some very beautiful girls who worked there. One of them was a lovely girl called Dale Wellhofer, the club's executive secretary and book-keeper, who was from New Jersey. One day, I walked into the front office to find Malcolm half sitting on Dale's desk, delivering a line that Omar Sharif would have been proud of. I sometimes thought Malcolm's talents were wasted in football. They would have got a much better platform in Hollywood.

'Dale,' he said, 'you're a very pretty girl. Tell me the best restaurant in Tampa, and Rodney and I will take you there for dinner tonight.'

A lot of women over the years have found Malcolm quite irresistible at times. Dale was no different and quickly accepted his invitation to Berns Steak House, not far from the stadium. It was, and still is, one of the best restaurants in South Florida. So off we go. Malcolm's got his date and I'm dragged along like a third wheel.

Apart from the excellent food, Berns' claim to fame is their wine list, which is the size of a telephone directory. At the time, the house policy was that if they couldn't provide your choice of wine because they were out of stock or for any other reason, they would serve you an alternative of similar quality free of charge. When this was confirmed by the waiter, Malcolm gave Dale a mischievous look and I sat back to watch the entertainment. Malcolm was a connoisseur when it came to champagne, and he perused the list as the waiter stood in front of him. Finally, he said, 'I see you have a 59 Cristal. We'll start with that.'

Footballers get a lot of stick for their lack of breeding, but Malcolm's Louis Roederer choice that night would have been worthy of royalty. The family-owned Grande Marque house, which was founded 200 years ago, produces some of the greatest champagne. Roederer's NV Brut Premier is considered consistently good but the prestige cuvee, Cristal, created for Tsar Alexander II in 1876, is one of the great luxury champagnes and because of its rarity and price it is not stocked by too many restaurants, which, of course, Malcolm knew only too well.

'Certainly, sir. Yes, I'm sure we can accommodate you,' replied the waiter. Five minutes later the champagne duly appeared along with the $280 bill, which today would be ten times that amount.

Malcolm's face was priceless as the waiter poured each of us a glass. Malcolm took a sip and in his London accent said knowledgeably, 'Yeah, lovely drop of stuff that Cristal, innit.' Then he picked up a steak knife, made an incision into the top of the cork, deftly inserted an American quarter coin and romantically presented it to Dale – pure class! Dale was touched and still has the cork to this day. After that evening, she had it mounted in a beautiful domed glass presentation display container which has a place of prominence in her lounge.

Life is funny. When you look back over the years you always seem to remember good times like that. On the outside, I guess I didn't look any different but emotionally I was entering the blackest period of my life, a deep abyss of depression that for a long, long time I never thought I could climb out of.

It started about a month after I arrived in Tampa. I woke up one morning and thought I'd made a catastrophic mistake coming to Florida. I don't know why, but I just couldn't free my mind of such dreadful feelings of melancholy. I was still struggling to come to terms with the way I had been dumped at Maine Road. I was also having a few problems settling in with the Rowdies. I had been made captain but I could tell it was more the decision of Beau Rogers than Eddie Firmani. After 11 days I chucked the armband in. My appointment had caused a few hassles with some of my team-mates which was followed by a disagreement over bonuses and I just couldn't be bothered with the aggravation.

Then there were days when I thought that soccer in America and the Rowdies would just collapse. Despite some of the fabulous players, I thought the standard overall was poor. Not many people had heard of me and from the point of view of being away from the spotlight, that was great, but I thought it was the end of my career. And football was all that I knew. Psychologically, I had lost it and I just didn't know which way to turn.

I thought I had made a desperate mistake taking my family to the States and even though I wasn't sure what to do, I asked Jean to take the kids back to England and set up home there. I was confused. I didn't know where I was going or where I'd end up. It must have been tough for her because she had only moved them there a few weeks earlier. I love my children more than anything in the world and it was the first time we had ever been apart. I was devastated but felt it was the right decision to make. I thought it was better for them to be away from me, away from the evil person that I thought I had become. Only after the separation could I, at last, make any sense of what was happening to me. Just over a year after my second spell with Fulham, we all emigrated to the USA for good, which turned out to be the best decision I could have made. My children ended up growing up in America and are American in all but name. They love living there.

After Jean returned to the UK, I put up the barriers once more to protect myself although I don't think many people noticed any difference in me. They would have if they'd seen me at night because then I would mostly climb into a bottle of vodka and drink until I collapsed into bed. That's what happened for the best part of 18 months.

Until then, I'd been pretty much a social drinker. The difference was that I had been in control. If I didn't want to drink, it didn't bother me and I never drank before a match in my life. But now my drinking was completely out of control, big-time.

I didn't drink in the morning, but as soon as training had finished I couldn't wait to have a few beers with the other players. After that, I would go to my apartment and sit by the pool with a bottle. It would be the same routine, day in and day out. It wasn't long before I was getting through a bottle a day. Looking back, it's astonishing how I could consume that much and still keep my fitness, but I did.

One afternoon towards the end of the season, I was lying on a lilo in the swimming pool, dreamily floating around with a Pina Colada in my hand, as you do, when the phone rang. I can remember it as clear as anything. It was a perfect Florida day with no humidity, just another day in paradise. I had half a mind not to bother answering it but the ringing went on and on. When I picked up the cordless receiver, I recognised the voice straightaway. It was Ken Adam, my agent.

'Hello, Ken,' I said. 'What's up?'

'Rod,' he replied. 'I've got a great offer for you.'

'Go on, then,' I said. 'Let's have it. '

When he said Fulham, I nearly fell in the pool laughing.

'No, listen,' Ken said. 'Fulham want you on loan for next winter. The English season starts in a month's time and you might find it interesting.'

I took a sip of the drink, adjusted my sunglasses and said, 'Ken, are you having a laugh? Why on earth would I want to go back to England? Especially to the Second Division.'

I had fond memories of Craven Cottage but I hadn't forgotten the rain, frost, snow and sludge of an English winter. When you're sitting in the sun with a cocktail in your hand, it takes a lot for you to be tempted by the likes of Hull, Carlisle and Hereford. Then Ken said five very tempting words – 'George Best's agreed to go.'

I immediately said another five – 'What time is the flight?'

I'd played against George with Manchester City and in America but I couldn't resist the chance of playing *with* him. Are you mad? I had always thought that Besty was the greatest player in the world. So that was the start of the three-ringed circus of me, George and dear old Bobby Moore at Fulham. The Rowdies were delighted with the arrangement too because it got me, their highest-paid player, off their payroll for their close season and they knew I would be fit when I returned.

After putting down the phone, I sat by the pool smiling to myself. You've got to follow your heart, wherever it leads.

and fergie thought united was a drinking club!

I love London Society! I think it has immensely improved. It is entirely composed now of beautiful idiots and brilliant lunatics. Just what society should be.

Oscar Wilde

Before I left for America in 1976, there wasn't a London league club ground where I hadn't played or scored. By the time I returned to Tampa after my stint at Fulham with Besty, there wasn't a London nightclub that I hadn't played at either. Highbury, Stamford Bridge, White Hart Lane? Forget it. To have seen the really great performances you had to have been at Tramp, Morton's or the Dover Street wine bar. What an incredible rollercoaster ride of a season that was! And we haven't even started talking about the football yet.

It was the season Liverpool rode roughshod over almost everybody on their way to the First Division championship and their first European Cup victory. I was really pleased for my Tampa team-mate Tommy Smith when he put Liverpool in front against Borussia Moenchengladbach. In Rome's Olympic Stadium, they had been drawing 1–1 and struggling a bit when Tommy, taking the place of the injured Phil Thompson, came to the rescue with a powerful headed goal to set up a 3–1 win. It was Tommy's farewell appearance for the club he had joined as a boy and what a way to go.

Tommy would have been a treble winner but for a fluke goal by Jimmy Greenhoff that gave Manchester United a 2–1 FA Cup final win over the Merseysiders the Saturday before. Greenhoff was trying to get out of the way of a Lou Macari shot but the ball struck him and flew over Ray Clemence's head and into an open goal – and poor old Bob Paisley missed out on a knighthood.

But the Tommy Docherty holding the FA Cup in the air in celebration of the Red Devils' resurrection must have been a different Tommy Docherty from the one who had spent less than a month at Loftus Road a few years earlier.

Incidentally, Besty left United the year before because he had been disillusioned by the way the club was going after Sir Matt Busby gave up the managership. He hated Tommy Docherty and used to joke that if the Doc said good morning, you had to 'go and check the effing weather!'

QPR played some great football that year, too. In Europe for the first time, they had scored 26 goals in four UEFA Cup ties and Stan Bowles, who hit 11 of them, broke the British record held by Dennis Viollet, Denis Law and Derek Dougan for scoring the most European goals in a season. I particularly remember watching Stan put on a terrific performance against Cologne and scoring a brilliant goal. He picked the ball up just outside the box, and dribbled past three defenders before walking the ball past a hypnotised German keeper and into the net. What a player Stan was! I've always felt he wasn't given the recognition he deserved.

Liverpool and Rangers were giving football fans value for money in the First Division but celebrities were turning up in their droves to watch Fulham in the Second. That year Craven Cottage was the original Planet Hollywood. Every week the stands would be full of pop stars and film stars plus all sorts of high flyers including politicians, businessmen and top inter-national models. You name 'em and they were there. Sometimes during a match, I would look up at the directors' box and more often than not it resembled a night at the Oscars! Going to a Fulham game became a fashionable thing to do. They came to see George, Bobby and me. Bobby retired at the end of that season after his 1,000th first-class match. After the game, we'd go off on the town with dozens of celebs in tow. It was the epitome of the roaring seventies.

My old mentor Alec Stock had signed George and me. After leaving QPR in 1968 he had gone to Luton for four years. Shortly after arriving at Kenilworth Road, he stole an unconvincing full-back called Malcolm Macdonald from Craven Cottage and turned him into one of the game's top strikers. That knack for spotting a bargain, which had also included me, was probably why Tommy Trinder persuaded him to join Fulham in 1972. There Alec had worked his usual magic, fusing great players who were coming to the end of their careers, such as Alan Mullery and Bobby Moore, with some talented youngsters. The result was Fulham's only appearance in an FA Cup final. Mooro led his new club to a 2–0 defeat by West Ham, his old club. But Alec Stock was still a winner because he had got Fulham all the way to Wembley and made a profit on the club's transfer dealings in the process.

Alec was in his mid fifties then and although he was never a technical football man, he was a superb judge of character, a kind of father figure who created the right environment for coaches and players to express their skills.

Alec got the ball rolling to bring George and me to Craven Cottage but it was Fulham directors Sir Eric Miller and Ernie Clay who put the deal together, assisted, of course, by Ken Adam, who also represented George at the time.

A few months before we went there, Fulham had been in a bit of a financial crisis after failing to get to grips with the building of a new riverside stand. In an early summer boardroom battle, Tommy Trinder lost out to Yorkshireman Clay, who had been introduced to the club by Sir Eric. An injection of new money quickly followed which enabled the club to sort out its cash-flow problems and get George and me on board. Tragically, Sir Eric later committed suicide in somewhat mysterious circumstances in the garden of his house. A businessman with diverse interests, he was under investigation by the fraud squad at the time of his death.

The first game I played for Fulham on my return was a League Cup match against Peterborough at Craven Cottage. It had been planned that George and I would make our debuts together but a bureaucratic cock-up in the transfer of his registration from the Aztecs meant that his first appearance was delayed for a week. So on 4 September, George, Bobby and I played our first league game together at home to Bristol Rovers. Previously the Craven Cottage gate had been below 10,000 but we ballooned it to over 21,000. The crowd didn't have to wait long to get their money's worth because Besty scored after just 71 seconds.

A few weeks later, on the day the red and yellow disciplinary card system was introduced, George was out in front again. He became one of the first players in the country to be shown a red card – for using foul and abusive language in a game against Southampton at the Dell. But what the hell! We were getting bigger gates at Craven Cottage, playing against teams like Hereford, than some First Division outfits.

I had agreed to go to Fulham without even asking how much the contract would be worth. Believe it or not I hadn't given it a thought. It was something I really wanted to do, so the money wasn't the most important factor. When the terms were explained to me shortly after I got there, I thought they were good. But when the Fulham bandwagon got going, it turned out to be nothing short of incredible. I was on a similar bonus system to the one I had been on at Manchester City – £100 per thousand people per game over the previous year's average. One week I got an extra £1,800, which was unheard of in those days.

If I was on that kind of pay-packet, imagine what George was getting. Besty was the star, with Bobby Moore and me playing supporting roles. It was worth it. Week after week, Craven Cottage was bulging at the seams and it was a very purple time.

I'll give you an example of the sort of thing that went on at Fulham in those mad days, which was all down to us three. Not long after we arrived, a Middle Eastern sheikh offered a staggering amount of money for Fulham to play an exhibition game in Saudi Arabia especially for his son. The one condition was that George, Bobby and I had to be in the line-up. Fulham turned it down at first but the sheikh wouldn't take no for an answer and came back with an incentive that Sir Eric and Ernie couldn't refuse.

So off we went and it turned into one of the most amazing trips I've ever had. The sheikh sent a Lear jet from his private fleet to collect us from Heathrow. As soon as I got on board I knew the Arabs had gone out of their way to please George because the stewardesses were the most stunning girls I'd ever seen. Then, as soon as the plane reached its cruising altitude, out came the Dom Perignon and there was Sir Eric doing the honours with the serving trolley. Naturally, George's was the first glass filled and I don't think it was empty for two days; nor was anyone else's for that matter. The sheikh was a fabulously hospitable host and spared no expense to make it comfortable for us. We played the game to a sell-out crowd in Dubai and, funnily enough, I can't remember what the score was or the name of the team we played against.

Arabs can be extraordinarily generous. At the after-match dinner I remarked how beautiful a gold-embossed glass serving tray was. I was just admiring it but the sheikh instantly gave it to me. The next day, I didn't feel I should admire the Rolls-Royce that he sent to take us on a tour of the city.

The flight back to the UK was something out of the movies. Again, as soon as the aircraft was airborne, it was champagne all the way – until we hit a mid-air crisis. Halfway home we ran out of champagne. George was mortified. We all were. Sir Eric walked straight up to the two pilots in their cabin and explained our predicament to them. I can still see them nodding earnestly as Sir Eric outlined his instructions. Within 30 minutes the jet was making an unscheduled stop so that more champagne could be picked up to tide us over until we reached London. Priceless! Back at Heathrow we practically fell off the plane, still clutching bottles of champagne . . . and bags of money. Crazy days!

Another time we went on a whistlestop tour of Norway where we were due to play two friendly games in five days. On arrival at Oslo's tiny airport, 5,000 screaming fans, mostly girls, welcomed us. They were all there to greet George, of course. We played the first game and won well. George scored, on the pitch as well, so it was off for a night on the town. It seemed like every fan who had been at the airport was in the nightclub we ended up in. The champagne was flowing and we were all having a brilliant time when suddenly George leaned across.

'Marshy,' he whispered in my ear. 'What time is the flight in the morning?' We were room-mates but I'd learned by now not to ask silly questions like why.

'10.15,' I told him. 'Don't be late.'

When the night fizzled out, I got a taxi back to the hotel with Mooro and Les Strong and left George to his own nocturnal devices. Hours later he stumbled into the hotel reception still repeating what he had desperately been drumming into his head all night – 'I can't miss the flight. I can't miss the flight.' At the concierge's desk, Besty got a withering look.

'I need a wake-up call for the morning,' he mumbled.

'Certainly, Mr Best. What time would you like it for?'

'7.30 on the button.'

The concierge glanced up condescendingly from his notepad.

'But Mr Best, it's twenty to eight now!'

Sir Eric idolised George and would have done almost any-thing for him. After every home game, he wouldn't miss a chat with George in the Duke of Wellington pub off the King's Road.

But halfway through the season, Alec Stock left Fulham. Years later he said in his autobiography that he knew things wouldn't work out the day Ernie Clay became chairman. I suppose it was obvious for everyone to see, really. No one had a greater reputation for honesty and decency in football than Alec.

Anyway, Bobby Campbell took over as manager. He had left Arsenal, where he had been coaching, to join Fulham in a similar capacity in the summer but he was not Alec's choice. I had a lot of time for Bobby and still do. I thought he was a cracking coach and a smashing bloke. So did George.

Bobby began his career in the 1960s with Liverpool, but played a few games only before moving on to Portsmouth, a club he later managed. Bobby had a reputation as a bit of a disciplinarian but, predictably, failed miserably with George in that respect. That's not a criticism – better coaches and managers than either Bobby or me have come to grief very quickly with Besty in that department.

In those days, Bobby was tee-total but Besty soon put a stop to that! When Bobby took over halfway through the season, we were beginning to lose touch with the top of the division. The reason for this was that although we could turn it on at home, our away form was rubbish. So Bobby decided that for the night before an away game, the whole team would stay at an hotel so that he could be sure George would be in a fit condition to play the next day. So what night did Bobby start this new plan for George? You couldn't make it up if you tried – New Year's Eve of course. You've got to laugh.

Our New Year's Day game was at Cardiff so Bobby booked the team into White's Hotel near Lancaster Gate. If George wasn't fit and fresh on the morning of the match, at least he would be on the team coach to Wales.

The curfew time was 10.30 p.m. and by then most of the players had already gone to bed. I was injured at the time but had gone along for the ride. Those who hadn't turned in, including Bobby Campbell, of course, Bobby Moore, physiotherapist Ron

Woolnough and Ernie Clay, were sitting in the hotel's lobby. At 10.45, Campbell decided to take a roll-call and there are no prizes for guessing the only person who wasn't there. So they waited and waited and waited. Eleven o'clock passed and still there was no George; nor was he there at 11.30, nor midnight. The manager looked bleakly at the floor and shook his head.

'Mooro,' he asked, 'where the hell can George be?' Bobby grinned wryly.

'There are four or five places he could be,' he said. 'I'll write you a list.'

When he handed it over, Campbell gulped. It was as long as your arm! Nevertheless, Clay and Campbell set off in Ernie's Rolls-Royce in search of George, and this time Bobby was determined to put Besty in his place. Down the list they went, from club to club, and all the time Bobby was rehearsing what he would say to George when he finally caught up with him.

'That's it, Besty,' he was saying. 'I've given you too many chances. This time I'm going to fine you ten thousand pounds. No, no, that won't do . . . George, I can't believe you've let the lads down like this . . . No, that won't work either.'

Two hours later they were still cruising around London and Bobby was still working on his verbal reprimand – 'This is it. You're effing useless, Besty. We're all sick of it. You're on your bike. It's the end, George. We're going to put you on the transfer list tomorrow . . .'

Finally, they got to Tramp, the last place on Mooro's list, and there sprawled across the bar completely legless was George.

'Right,' said Bobby to Ernie. 'Leave it to me.'

Like a man on a mission, Campbell strode up to George and put his hand on his shoulder.

'Er, George,' Bobby said nervously. 'What are you having? Would you mind if we joined you?'

The three of them looked at each other and burst out laughing. Bobby and Ernie stayed with George until about four in the morning and when they all got back to the hotel, Bobby was as drunk as George. And that was Bobby's method of disciplining Besty! Coming back from Cardiff the following night, Bobby sat at the front of the coach and said nothing. It wasn't the 3–0 loss that left him speechless – he couldn't work out why George was sitting there comfortably doing a crossword while he had a blinding hangover.

From then on, Bobby and George got on famously. George liked Bobby because he wasn't bossy like a lot of managers had tried to be with him. He didn't worry too much about what George and I did before a game, either – just so long as we did the business on the pitch the next day.

However, he still thought he had to make his point to George, so he tried a different approach. Before the next home game he went looking for George and found him in the Duke of Wellington, chatting to a couple of girls. Bobby joined them and stayed for a couple of hours, having a good time. At closing time, he offered George a lift back to the team's hotel, but instead of going straight there, he drove to a Greek restaurant where Sir Eric was having a party. He kept George there till about five in the morning before taking him back to the hotel and escorting him to his room. At the door Bobby looked him straight in the eye and said, 'You'd better play well today. If you don't, I'll have your bollocks.' George played a blinder.

After that we all got on like a house on fire and Bobby used to join George, Mooro, Sir Eric and me at the Duke of Wellington for a post-match drink although he used to have Coke.

For the first half of the season we had been brilliant, absolutely fantastic. For the first 10 weeks or so we looked set for promotion. On away trips I'd room with George. We always got on well and most of the time we behaved ourselves. We also found time to do some television work, which I really enjoyed.

The highest position we reached in the Second Division was fourth and the 4–1 win over Hereford that took us there was a classic. When I say that, I mean it was a classic for fun. I scored twice but after that George had the ball so much I had to tackle him myself just to get a kick. Then George did the same to me and on it went. Everyone in the crowd was roaring with laughter and that's how it continued. Our Showbiz XI brought back the entertainment that had been sadly missing for some years. Even the referees and officials joined in.

But what goes up comes down. Fulham's nose-dive started with a 2–0 defeat by Chelsea in front of a 55,000 crowd at Stamford Bridge just before Christmas. George, unfortunately, got another red card in that game for a wrist gesture to the referee similar to the one that contributed to his sending off at Southampton.

After that, Fulham lost nine of the next 12 matches and plunged from ninth to 20th spot. It finally went pear-shaped for both George and me towards the end of February. I had been struggling with torn ligaments in my right ankle. It was an injury that was much worse than the medical people at Craven Cottage thought, and I had been out for a couple of months. What really annoyed me was that I kept telling them how bad it was but they didn't seem to listen. The ankle remains swollen to this day.

George had been injured, too. After a bender at Tramp, he had crashed a Fiat that belonged to the chairman's daughter into a lamp-post outside Harrods. Well, if you're going to have a bang, you've got to do it in style, haven't you? George's head went right through the windscreen, cutting his face to pieces, and he also fractured a shoulder blade. Fifty-seven stitches were needed around his forehead and eyes and you can still see some of the scars. The doctors said he would be out for four months. George was back in five weeks.

Besty was beginning to get unhappy about a few things. He told me that some of the financial promises Fulham had made hadn't been kept. I knew about some of that because it had taken them ages to come up with my signing-on fee.

Besty was also disappointed that the flat the club had promised him turned out to be a dump. When his then wife Angie joined him from Beverly Hills where she had been working for the singer Cher, they had a falling out about it. Angie moved out and went to work for the Playboy Club, which was a bad thing at the time for George I think.

I felt Fulham had let me down because I hadn't been getting the proper medical treatment and they also reneged on a bonus. I could have taken them to arbitration but I just wanted to get away because I wasn't enjoying the football any more. You never do when you're not fully fit. The glamour had started to wear off and it was a miserable time.

Jean and I were still separated and she had moved into a house in Twickenham with the children. I frequently visited and often stayed, but my drinking hadn't subsided one little bit. How could it with the King's Road company I was keeping?

Surrounded by so much razzmatazz and earning very good money, you would have thought I might have forgotten the Manchester City nightmare, but I hadn't. I just couldn't get the experience out of my head or come to terms with the way my situation had been handled. As I've said, I knew I had been at the top of my game at the time but the humiliation, embarrassment even, of what had occurred was so deep-rooted that I felt I couldn't cope. I couldn't even pick up a newspaper and read about City. The year I left, they had won the League Cup, beating Newcastle 2–1, and while I was at Fulham they had given Liverpool a run for the championship, finishing runners-up by a point.

I was genuinely pleased for some of the guys, Colin Bell for instance. At the time he was making a comeback after the horrific knee injury he sustained in a game against Manchester United in the November of 1975. Set free by Dennis Tueart, Bell went on one of his characteristic runs towards the United penalty area. As Martin Buchan tried to cut him off, Bell dragged the ball back and around him. But his studs became stuck in the ground and under the weight of Buchan's challenge, Colin fell, bursting an artery and a blood vessel in his knee. I well remember the agony on his face as they stretchered him off.

Colin was one of the finest footballers I have ever seen, let alone played alongside. Most people think of him as a runner – he was even nicknamed 'Nijinsky' after the racehorse – but he was much more than that. On the pitch, he didn't show off the repertoire of tricks that he was capable of. He could do most of the things I could do – flicks and drag backs, that sort of thing. The reason was that he had such a great footballing brain that he used tricks only when he felt he had to; otherwise he thought they were unnecessary.

Malcolm Allison had made Bell City's record purchase when they paid Bury £45,000 for him in 1966. Malcolm told me that at the time there was quite a bit of interest in Bell and to get him, City had to take out a bank loan to pay for the deal. While the loan was being arranged, Malcolm was so scared he would lose Bell that he would go to watch him play for Bury and tell other coaches and scouts things like, 'He can't play, he's no good in the air and he has a hopeless left foot.' As soon as the money became available, Malcolm had his man in a flash.

Bell had sheer class and he became the heartbeat of those great City sides of the 1960s and 1970s. It was a privilege to play alongside him and to be his captain. I hope that he is remembered for all the great things he did and not for his famous appearance as a second-half substitute for Bobby Charlton in the 1970 World Cup quarter-final against West Germany in Mexico when we were 2–0 up and lost 3–2.

Fulham were desperate for me to return to the team with George and, in my opinion, I was brought back far too soon for a game against Wolverhampton at Molineux. It was a typical bleak February Midlands day with a bitter, sleet-filled north-easterly wind. The pitch was a mixture of snow and ankle-deep mud.

When I got out there, I was frozen to the marrow and never warmed up. George had spent the previous season in California and I had been in the sunshine state of Florida, so this type of game was definitely not up our alley.

Halfway through the second half we found ourselves 5–0 down, which was no real surprise to anyone watching. Besty was playing badly, I was crap, Fulham was crap. After their fifth goal had gone in, our goalkeeper Gerry Peyton picked the ball out of the net and booted it up to the halfway line where Besty and I were standing in the swamp of the centre circle, waiting for the seventh kick-off of the afternoon. We watched the ball through the pouring rain as it bombed down towards us. Moments later it covered us with mud as it landed and it hadn't even bounced. For a moment we didn't say a word. George slowly wiped the muck from his face with both hands and called out to me.

'Hey, Marshy,' he said. 'What the fuck are we doing here?'

'You're dead right,' I said. 'This is bollocks.'

Two weeks later I was back in Florida.

CHAPTER 7

tears of a clown prince

Footballers are no different than human beings.

Graham Taylor, Watford and former England
manager

Imagine this if you can. At around four on a rainy morning, a car is hurtling along one of London's busiest roads. Inside the vehicle, a man, gripping the steering wheel with an intensity that has turned his knuckles white, peers past the windscreen wipers at a road he can barely see. His brain is so addled with alcohol and depression that he can picture no way ahead in his life either. So in desperation he stamps on the accelerator and sends a fashionable Mini Cooper flashing through set after set of red traffic lights. Is it a nightmare or a maniac with a death wish in a Hollywood movie? It was neither. It actually happened and the driver of the car was me.

Before I went back to Tampa for my second stint with the Rowdies, I was so desperate with depression I could hardly think straight. I was sharing a flat with Malcolm Allison and Serena Williams in London's Cromwell Road and most people thought I was still the same old cheeky chappie I had always been, still clubbing it and enjoying the laughs. If there was a smile on my face it was, as Smokey Robinson says, there just to fool the public. Deep down inside I was morose and unable to come to

111

terms with the end of my playing career at the top level. I was out of control. I had completely lost life's plot and was as low as I had ever been. I couldn't see any way out. There didn't seem to be a light at the end of the tunnel and I didn't really know why I was feeling that way.

On the night with the car I had been on a bender from hell. You name it and I probably drank it – vodka, champagne, brandy, everything. George and I had started at the Duke of Wellington before doing the usual round of clubs and wine bars and ending up at Tramp. At three in the morning, Besty had gone on somewhere else, leaving me boring Johnny Gold, Tramp's owner. I was probably mumbling and babbling incoherently so all credit to Johnny for being so patient. Finally, he offered to get me a limo home but I refused saying that I was going to drive myself. He tried to stop me but couldn't.

Now I've done some daft things in my life but what I did next was probably the most stupid thing any person could do. I got into the Mini and headed off to see Jean. I'm embarrassed to admit to it now. Not only was I blind drunk, I was also not myself mentally. As I turned the car on to the Cromwell Road, I truly felt that I did not want to go on. I just simply didn't care whether I lived or died.

I replayed in my head the comments of some of my so-called pals at Manchester City and their betrayal hit me hard all over again. As I hurtled through London, I could see the traffic signals turn red as I approached them but I drove through anyway. I must have shot past at least half a dozen. I was half hoping a car would hit me and end it all. I suppose I was clinically depressed. When you are like that, you don't think rationally.

Fortunately, I didn't go all the way out to Twickenham. I went straight to Malcolm's flat where I collapsed on the bed. I was very lucky not to have hit anybody or caused an accident. I could have killed someone. But, at the time, it was as though it was someone else driving that car, not me at all. It shook me up, but it didn't stop me drinking and the next night I was back on the sauce. This time, however, I took a taxi home.

I returned to Florida from Fulham in a blaze of publicity and my first appearance for the Rowdies was in an indoor game against Leningrad, who were on a tour of the States, in St Petersburg before a sell-out crowd. It was a brilliant match in which I scored five but we lost 8–7. Even so, I was voted the game's Most Valuable Player, which annoyed me because I believed, and still do, that the award should go to someone on the winning side. I went straight to the locker room without waiting for the presentation and showered. I was so mad that we had lost that I didn't want to speak to anybody. The Rowdies were none too happy and fined me my match fee of $1,000.

Before the season was very much older, I'd upset a few more Tampa officials. I had another major bust-up with Eddie Firmani, which led to me walking out of the club. Firmani went to the owners and demanded that either I went or he did. Eventually, he did. Before then, I agreed to come back after certain clauses in my contract had been explained to Eddie.

I was very pleased to be back in the warm weather, though, and the Rowdies medical team got my ankle back into shape very quickly indeed. Sports medical treatment in America is streets ahead of anything in the UK and it wasn't long before my ankle was much better although the swelling did not go completely. Swimming in the 75 degree Gulf of Mexico in the afternoons helped as well.

Football-wise, things were great during the 1977 season. The NASL had gone from strength to strength and some of the team line-ups looked like they had been picked from a Who's Who of football stars with German aces Franz Beckenbauer, Gerd Muller and Paul Breitner now on the scene.

My crowning glory was when we beat the New York Cosmos 5–1 in Tampa Stadium. At the time, the Cosmos team included Pele, Beckenbauer, Carlos Alberto and former Coventry player

Dave Clements. Dave had been kicking me all night but I had a magnificent first half in spite of his attentions. However, in the second half, he went too far. When he committed another horrible foul on me with the referee again taking no action, I'd had just about as much as I could take. So I decided to get my own back. Moments later, I received a pass and when Dave came in from behind, I elbowed him straight in the face. Then, after moving away, I turned to face him and brought the house down by taunting him matador-style with the ball between my knees.

Pele went berserk at this. I've already said what a sublime player he was but he also had a very physical side to his game. At the sight of my antics, he ran over and launched himself in my direction. I can still see the look of anger in his eyes. He grabbed hold of my head and dug his finger in my ear, which started to bleed. The pictures of this clash were splashed in the sports sections of every American newspaper the following day.

That incident apart, it had been a superb exhibition of football, watched not only by the 55,000 full house, but by millions on coast-to-coast television, something that is very rare even today.

But it wasn't the end of our little feud and in the re-match, in front of a 77,000 capacity crowd in the Giants' Stadium, Pele had another go at me. I had been up to my usual tricks with the ball and he caught me very high with both feet. It was like being hit by an Exocet missile. Both of us tumbled on to the running track around the pitch. I thought it was clearly a red-card case but when we got up I was astonished to see the referee wave play on without even booking the great man. The referee was Gordon Hill from Kirby Muxloe, Leicestershire, whom I already knew well from my Football League days.

'Hey, Gordon,' I shouted. 'What was that? What are you going to do?'

Gordon stood there for a moment with his hands on his hips shaking his head. Then he looked up at the crowd who were roaring their approval of his inaction and said, 'What do you want me to do, Rodney? Send him off?' Ducking the debris that was now being thrown down at me, I guessed he was right.

Gordon had got it wrong in my first game against Arsenal for Manchester City at Highbury in 1973. It was 0–0 at the time and from a throw-in just outside the Arsenal box, I controlled the ball with my thigh before bicycle-kicking it over my head towards the goal's far post. The hopeful cross-cum-shot beat the Gunners' goalkeeper, Jimmy Rimmer, and crashed on to the corner of the woodwork. Then it bounced back into play off Rimmer's arm as Franny Lee came diving in to bullet a header towards the other side of the goal. It looked a certain winner until Arsenal's centre-half Jeff Blockley appeared from nowhere and blatantly punched the ball out of play. Nobody at Highbury had seen a more obvious penalty, except Gordon who missed it and gave a corner kick instead. I lost my rag and as Gordon came running past me to take his position at the far post, I grabbed him around the throat with both hands and tried to throttle him. Some of the other players pulled me off. In his autobiography, Gordon admitted that when I reacted like that it made him think that he might have got that one a bit wrong.

The Rowdies reached the playoffs again in 1977 but the Cosmos at last got their revenge, beating us 3–0 in the first round. After our defeat there was nobody to stop New York and they eventually won the Soccer Bowl by beating Seattle 2–1. That season had been the most successful ever for the NASL. Attendances were up by over a third and the average playoff gate was over 30,000. New York averaged 57,000 that season and for one Rowdies v. Cosmos game, 62,394 people turned up. The Cosmos topped that figure a few weeks later with a 67,691 crowd for a match against the Strikers.

But the best crowd was saved for the last match of the year when an astonishing 75,000 fans braved a driving rainstorm to watch Pele's final exhibition game for New York against Santos, the only other club team he had appeared for. In the Giants' Stadium, Pele played one half for each side and it was fitting that he gave the Cosmos a 2–1 win with a stunning free kick. It was a marvellous send-off for a 22-year career. No wonder he cried like a baby when he left the pitch. Rightly called the greatest player who has ever lived, his goal tally for Santos of 1,090 in 1,114 games will never be beaten.

Looking back, I sometimes wonder how I could have played as well as I did during that period. Jean and the kids came over to stay for a while but I was still drinking the best part of a bottle of vodka a day. I guess you've got to be fit to do it in the first place.

After the 1977 American season ended, I went back to London and it was a very lonely period for me. It was my first winter without a club and I didn't know what to do with myself. I spent most of the time boozing and plumbing the depths of despair over the end of my British career. The sessions became almost daily before and after I had moved out of Malcolm's place and bought a flat of my own. I particularly remember one night when I drank myself into oblivion once more. It was a very serious all-nighter with Allison and we did the usual round of pubs and nightspots before finally ending up at the Playboy Club. Malcolm loved to gamble. I was happy with a drink.

I recall staring at the roulette wheel as it spun and the next thing I knew I was waking up the following afternoon lying on top of my bed with all my clothes on – overcoat, shoes, unshaven, the lot. I felt awful, degraded even. 'Christ,' I said to myself. 'You've completely lost it, mate.'

Aside from the chance to play football again, I had hoped that the move to America would make my marriage stronger. It had suffered under the strain of everything that had happened and I had thought that if we could get away from the goldfish bowl existence of Manchester and start afresh in a new country where nobody knew me, it might help. But I'd sent Jean and the kids home; and rather than helping the situation, all I succeeded in doing was creating a new monster over there. I was on every TV programme, in the paper every day and became the most recognisable sportsman in the Florida area.

I was incredibly low and I've come to the conclusion that I got the way I did because of the way I am. I blamed myself completely for having to leave City and I was punishing myself for what I saw as my failure but also I was still very angry at being let down by people whom I had hoped would stand by me. I became very down on myself and this was having a major effect on my relationship with Jean and the kids. I was still so wrapped up in it that there was no room for anyone else in my life. Of course, the drink was a major factor. I was out of it most of the time and far from getting away from the high life, I was as active as ever. I just couldn't stop drinking.

Jean has commented that from the day I left Manchester City, and for the best part of the next two years I was a different person. She was so saddened to watch me go through it knowing there wasn't a lot anyone could do for me. It was just something that I had to sort out for myself.

When we were apart I would always come to see the children, as I missed them. And I made sure that they never went without anything. They had a nice home and even though I was going through a horrible time myself, I still tried to put them first. But I know I often seemed in a bad way mentally when I went to see them.

Jean never had any time for Malcolm Allison and was very pleased when I bought a place of my own. She didn't blame Malcolm for what happened to me, but felt that he didn't help me. She thought all the heavy drinking sessions just made me worse and that Malcolm was the wrong sort of person for me to be around at the time. All I was doing was drinking and I lost weight because I wasn't eating properly.

I needed professional help. It's difficult to tell someone who is depressed what to do and all people would say to me was 'pull yourself together'. You can't make sweeping statements about what the best course is for someone else, particularly a top footballer. Everything seems to be on an intense level. If a guy goes to work as a salesman and has a great week, the only people who know about it are the 30 or 40 people he works with and his family at home. Similarly, if he has a nightmare week, doesn't sell a thing, then goes home and has a row with his wife, falling down drunk in the street on the way, it's the same people who know about it. But in football, everybody knows what you do. If you score a hat-trick, it's all over the papers; and if you fall over drunk, it's an even bigger story. Everything is magnified and the extremes of situations like that make them so difficult to deal with. All sorts of modern stars, like Stan Collymore and Paul Gascoigne, know this to their cost.

Nobody got it worse than Besty, though. Even today he can't go anywhere without a camera being pushed in his face. Sometimes he has other things pushed in his face, too, like a glass or a bottle when just having a quiet drink. There's always some nutcase who wants to make a name for himself. George has been under the microscope for most of his life. Perhaps that's why he has drunk himself into oblivion for 30 years, as an escape from the artificially imposed pressures of life.

If your face is well known, some people think they own you. They don't even look at you as if you are a human being. A few years ago I went to a restaurant with Jean, and the owner walked up to me and cut off my tie, without saying a word. Apparently, it was the custom of the house to hang the ties of celebrities on the wall but nobody bothered to explain it to me. At the time I was in a bad mood, irritable, like everybody can be. Luckily, Jean managed to steer me out of trouble. You see how easy it is to get in the newspapers for all the wrong reasons.

Not long after I returned to Tampa to prepare for the 1978 season, I woke up one morning with a terrible backache. I

TEARS OF A CLOWN PRINCE

thought I had pulled a muscle in training the previous day so I immediately went for treatment. It got a little better but not much. I tried to train a few days later but it kept recurring.

Tampa's medical people advised me to see a back specialist, which I did. I was given a thorough examination and a body scan. Afterwards, the doctor called me in and asked me if I drank a lot. I said no, not really, just socially. He asked what I called socially and what I called social drinking.

I don't know why but for some reason I decided to admit what had been going on for the past 18 months or so and it was one of the best decisions I've made in my life. I confessed to the doctor just how much I had been boozing and I didn't hold back. I came straight out with it and said I had been drinking at least four or five bottles a week. For a moment the doctor was silent as he studied my charts. When he looked up from them I got the biggest shock of my life.

'Your liver is one and a half times the size of a normal one,' he said. 'If you don't stop drinking like that, you'll be dead before you're forty.'

I was stunned. My knees were actually shaking when I left the clinic. It was a diagnosis I never expected. What the doctor said shook me completely. I hadn't realised just how much I was out of control. For a long time after that, I was stone cold sober; and I never went back to that level of drinking again. One of the first things I did was to phone Jean. By the following year we were back together again.

Perhaps it was the shock treatment I needed. I have sometimes been asked why I was able to control the drinking and Besty wasn't. I find that difficult to answer, even though George and I have spoken about it. Once I told him about this time in my life, when I couldn't manage my drinking. He didn't say anything, but George has always been very supportive and I hope he can say the same about me.

Back with the Rowdies, Gordon Jago had taken over from

Eddie Firmani. I had always got on well with Gordon, ever since my days with him at Queens Park Rangers, and one of the first things he did was make me captain.

Gordon always came across as a very upright and serious man, but he could be hilarious when he wasn't even meaning to be. I can remember preparing for a game in San Diego. He was giving a team-talk in the gardens of the hotel. Dressed in a suit, he was sitting crosslegged on a backless bench with his hands wrapped around his knees, rocking gently backwards and forwards. Suddenly, he fell over backwards and his legs went right over his head. Yet he jumped up in an instant and carried on talking as if nothing had happened. His hair was covered in grass and he looked just like Peter Sellers' Inspector Clouseau. David Robb, the former Aberdeen striker, and I were crying hysterically with laughter.

That season the NASL decided to expand in a big way. Six more teams were added and the divisional line-up was changed to two conferences, each comprising three divisions. This increased the number of games to 30. More players arrived from the UK. The Philadelphia Fury signed Alan Ball, and George Graham went to the California Surf. The biggest coup of the time was by the Express who lured Trevor Francis to Detroit for a summer loan period not long after he had become Britain's first million-pound player.

Yet just as the NASL was on the verge of becoming one of the biggest footballing stages in the world, I could see storm clouds gathering on the horizon. I think change is essential but in football you can't have one set of rules for one country and another for the rest of the world.

The NASL first upset FIFA by retaining controversial rule changes including shoot-outs for draws, the 35-yard offside line and bonus points for goals scored. Not only that, there were occasions when the League ignored regulations that governed the world's transfer system, which antagonised UEFA. Before long, the NASL had alienated itself from both of the game's ruling bodies.

The League ignored other warning signs. Although the Cosmos' attendances were still around 48,000 after Pele left, most games that didn't involve them, with the exception of the Whitecaps and the Rowdies, showed a worrying decline.

The Rowdies were still on a high. We won our championship that year and our two-legged playoff semi-final was against the Fort Lauderdale Strikers, whom George had joined from the Aztecs. The Strikers won the first game 3–2 but we captured the second 3–1. We were tied because goal aggregate didn't count in the United States then; nor was there extra time. Instead, a 30-minute mini-game had to be played, followed by a shoot-out if necessary.

During the mini-game, which ended 0–0, the Strikers coach Ron Newman substituted George which meant he could not take part in the shoot-out. As he left the field, Besty was livid and he showed it by throwing his soaking wet shirt right into Newman's face. The Tampa crowd went ballistic. There was almost a riot because they'd never seen anything like it before. In America, a coach is generally idolised and treated with the utmost respect.

I scored the winning goal in the shoot-out, but we lost to the Cosmos in the Soccer Bowl. It had been a brilliant season nonetheless. I was voted on to the NASL All-Star team for a second time. It read: Kevin Keelan; Carlos Alberto, Mike England, Ray Evans; Chris Turner, Franz Beckenbauer, Gerry Daly, Rodney Marsh; Mike Flanagan, Trevor Francis, Giorgio Chinaglia.

At the start of the 1979 season, as my life was at last getting back into shape, American soccer began to fragment. In my opinion, it all started to go south the moment Ed Garvey, a former executive director of American football's NFL and a lawyer, became involved in setting up a players' association. At the time, the game's popularity in the States was at its highest and this had led to a huge TV contract. Although I thought most players in the NASL were underpaid, I was very worried about the consequences of Garvey's involvement. A lot of businessmen were beginning to be concerned about how big soccer was getting and I think they viewed it as a threat. For instance, attendances for baseball's New York Yankees, American sport's Manchester United, were about 30,000, but the Cosmos would regularly get as many as 70,000 for one of their games. I never felt soccer came first with Garvey.

However, before the season began he successfully lobbied all the NASL players to form an association. When he came to Tampa, I became convinced that he was only interested in the business side of things and not in how to sustain and build on the increased interest in soccer. Garvey told us how successful a collective bargaining agreement had been for the NFL players and he persuaded us to sign an agreement backing whatever decision the association, or Garvey as its boss, made. I now feel that was a big mistake.

The first thing he did was call a one-day strike for 14 April. It was the day the Rowdies were due to play the Cosmos before a sell-out 70,000 crowd and a live NBC television audience at the Giants' Stadium. All the players backed Garvey but the games went ahead when the clubs fielded scabs – amateurs and kids from the parks.

It's true we all got more money, and the players' salary cap was abolished, but it pushed a wedge between us and the club owners, which led to a lot of squabbling between all parties concerned. Eventually, the NASL lost its extremely lucrative television contract and as a result of that the League's income was so severely damaged that it could not support the increased costs.

All this didn't deter some teams from mortgaging their futures to buy the best talent they could afford. The Cosmos, with the deep pockets of Warner Brothers to call upon, carried on throwing money around. Then the Aztecs, playing catch-up, got into the act by giving Johan Cruyff almost a million pounds to come out of retirement.

Three months after the season started, I decided to hang up my boots; or to be more accurate, my arm was twisted to pack it in. Beau Rogers had left the club and the new general manager was a guy called Chas Seredneski. My love–hate relationship with the Rowdies had continued unabated. Seredneski wanted me out because he thought I was becoming too powerful and too influential. It was a situation not too dissimilar to David Ginola's when he was at Spurs, but the Rowdies were winning championships.

One afternoon Seredneski called me into his office and told me that as I was 35 the club did not want to renegotiate my contract which would be up at the end of the season. The problem the Rowdies had was that I had become so popular with the fans that they couldn't just get rid of me. The publicity would have been horrendous for them. So Seredneski offered me a testimonial worth five times my salary. It was a huge dilemma for me, especially as it was the first to be offered to a soccer player in the States. Reluctantly, I decided to accept but I felt it was blackmail really. By giving me a benefit game, the Rowdies got rid of me without it costing them a penny. But that's all part of football, which I understand.

Before the testimonial I had one more competitive game to play. We had had another brilliant season, again winning our divisional championship, and my last match would be the Soccer Bowl against the Vancouver Whitecaps in the Giants' Stadium. Just like my four-year playing career with Tampa, it was a sweet and sour occasion.

The guest of honour in New York was Henry Kissinger and as captain I got to have a long chat with him. As I expected, he knew nothing about the game and for him it was a public relations exercise. Kissinger thought he knew what he was talking about but he didn't have a clue. I suppose you could call him the Richard Caborn of America.

The game was very tight but thanks to Alan Ball, who was now with the Whitecaps, and the former Ipswich striker Trevor Whymark, Vancouver had a 2–1 second-half lead. The final amazing moment of my playing career came with 10 minutes left. I'd never been substituted in my life for reasons other than injury, so when I looked up to see my No. 10 being held up, I was astonished – mortified even. I couldn't believe Gordon Jago would do that and as I walked off I was fuming. When I got to the dug-out, I threw my shirt on the floor and said, 'Gordon. It's my last game. Why the fuck have you taken me off?'

He looked at me and said, 'Well, to be honest, Rod, I thought we needed a bit more pace up front.'

'Gordon,' I said. 'How long have you known me? Fifteen years? With ten minutes of my career left you've realised that I'm not fucking quick enough?!'

When Graham Taylor ended Gary Lineker's England career in Sweden in a similar way, I knew exactly how Gary felt.

But in my testimonial a week later, I got a super send-off in spite of a tremendous thunderstorm that threatened to wreck the evening. The Tampa fans were brilliant and more than 20,000 turned up for a great match against the Fort Lauderdale Strikers. It was a very emotional evening for me and when the game finished I couldn't resist a passing shot at the press. They weren't going to get rid of me that easily. After the final whistle blew I walked straight into the press box and made an announcement – 'I can make you a promise,' I told them. 'I'll be back.' And I was determined to keep it.

From my playing days, I've only got a few regrets. One is when I broke someone's leg in a League Cup game for Manchester City against Rochdale. We were beating them 7–0 at Maine Road and I was playing really well. All evening, though, one of their defenders was trying to kick lumps off me. I could have walked away from the situation because we were winning easily but for some reason I chose not to. With a few minutes remaining, the ball bounced between me, this defender and one of his team-mates so I went in high intending to do him. Unfortunately, I missed and hit the team-mate instead, snapping his leg. He was carried off on a stretcher in agony and immediately rushed to hospital.

I bitterly regret it to this day. After the game, I went straight from the ground to the hospital with Willie Donachie and asked permission to see the lad. When I was allowed in, I told him how sorry I was and how I couldn't apologise enough. Well, the kid looked up at me and said, 'Rod, can I have your autograph. I've been dying to meet you.' I signed his programme but it still chokes me that I broke another professional's leg.

Jean had the last word on my retirement as a player. I've always tried to keep football and family life separate and before my testimonial she chose to give her one and only interview to a newspaper. She said:

I didn't agree with Rod retiring when he did. I think the club treated him shabbily really. I think they should have talked him into staying. I tried and possibly the club could have talked him into it.

In a playoff game against San Diego which lasted 135 minutes, players younger than Rod went off with cramp but he hung on in there.

It's got beyond emotion for me. I was alone after Rodney told me he was retiring and I got truly upset. Sad? Yes, I am, because I think it is wrong. It affects me more than him. The things I read in the paper bother me at times. I find it difficult to cope with. One or two people accused him of not fighting in the Soccer Bowl game and that really got me. Here's a man who has played for his country and this was the most important game of his life. People who said he didn't try killed me.

I've only seen him play four times and they've all been with the Rowdies. But I'm glad he's kept home life and football apart. I strongly believe he is very different at home from on the field. The character you see is, as someone once said, a playboy. But at home he enjoys nothing more than swimming in the pool with the kids.

When I look back over our life, all the experiences have been good. What I've enjoyed most is that life has never been dull.

CHAPTER 8

coaching my way in the usa

*Everyone has pressure, whatever walk of life they are in. I
happen to like the aggravation that goes with football
management – it seems to suit my needs.*

Graeme Souness, Blackburn Rovers manager

If I told you I got my first job in US football management in 1980
because I had been one of the biggest names in soccer you
probably wouldn't be that surprised. But it wouldn't be true. The
only qualification needed to become assistant coach of the semi-
professional team New York United was the ability to speak
English! I don't think they had anyone in the front office who
could do that. You can imagine the chaos that caused when
organising the season's fixtures, for instance.

That's one of the things that make football so different in
America. The longest distance you travel for an away game in
Britain is around 400 miles. In the States, it can be 4,000.

After retiring from Tampa, I thought clubs would be queuing
up for me to coach or manage their team but six months later the
phone had hardly rung. Then, unexpectedly, I got a call from the
owner of United, a Long Island side. His name was Vincent
Scotto and he was a wealthy Italian restaurateur.

As I've always liked pizza – and it was the only offer – I
thought I'd give it a try. When I got there, I found that I had

been appointed without the knowledge of the head coach, Gil Mardesescu, a former Romanian international. I was expecting that to be a problem but he didn't seem to care too much, and we only communicated in sign language.

What a baptism in management it was! The team had already done pre-season training. A couple of days after I arrived, Vinny told me he was giving a party at one of his restaurants two days before our first game of the season in Sacramento. Before returning to New York a week later, we were also scheduled to play another two matches in California. It's what they call being 'on the road' in American sport.

When I turned up for the bash at Scotto's, the place was already jumping. Everyone involved with the team was there. We sat down to a beautiful Italian meal with gallons of wine. Every player was given a bag that contained a club suit and tracksuit. It was a typical Italian night with loads of speeches, all theatrically delivered as only Italians can. Everyone was hugging and kissing and emotionally wishing each other good luck for the season. Money appeared to be no object. At the end of the evening, about 11 o'clock, Vinny called me over.

'Rodney,' he said in broken English. 'I want you to have a great time on the West Coast. Everything is down to you. You are in charge of the trip. You can take eighteen players. Buona fortuna.'

'Haven't you discussed this with the head coach?' I asked.

'No. You can do that now,' Vinny answered.

'But we're leaving tomorrow,' I said. Vinny looked at me and laughed.

'Here's my credit card,' he said. 'You take care of it. Spend as much as you have to. There's no limit.'

Then it dawned on me that nobody at the club had booked the plane tickets or any hotels. On the Friday night before Sunday's game, not a thing had been done. I thought he was winding me up for a laugh, but he wasn't.

So there and then, Ann Capabianco, the team's executive secretary and daughter of one of the directors, and I started on the job of organising the trip. Firstly, I went to the head coach and we selected which players to take. Then we had to tell them. Ann and I were up all night phoning airlines and hotels before meeting at New York's La Guardia Airport the next morning. We got nine players on one flight, three on another and so on until we were all on our way, at different times, to California. It was a nightmare.

By the time we left, not all the hotels had been booked. Ann finished doing that while I was in the air and I didn't know who was in which hotel until I phoned her after touching down.

Amazingly, we won all our three games and came back heroes. But what an experience. Until then, I had been used to being the star and having everything done for me. Now I was doing everything, including carrying the bags. Who says I've got a big ego?

We had a great season, even playing in the Shea Stadium where the Beatles had made such a memorable appearance 15 years earlier. Fifty-five thousand screaming fans showed up in the baseball arena to see the Fab Four; we got 1,500 and I thought the whole thing was a joke. Half the pitch was in the red ochre baseball diamond.

I got on famously with everyone at New York United, except the general manager. Isn't there always one? I had been at the club three months when one day at training he came up to me with five Uruguayan refugees and said, 'Here you are, Rodney. These guys will join in.'

I asked him what he was talking about. He said he had just signed them and was in the process of getting their residency papers sorted out. As assistant coach, I told him in no uncertain terms that this wasn't the way things were done.

'No,' he said. 'You don't get it. I'm the general manager and this is what we are going to do.'

'OK,' I said. 'Do it your fucking self then.'

The next day I was packed and on the first plane back to London. I'd started in management as I was to go on. I didn't tolerate interference then and I never have.

When I retired from playing at Tampa, Jean and the kids moved back to England. We hadn't separated again or anything like that. I just thought that it was better for Joanna and Jonathan to be settled because although I didn't have any doubts about my ability as a football man, I wasn't sure how it would turn out.

But I wasn't unemployed for long. A few weeks after I returned to the UK, I got a phone call from someone who said he was acting for a new football franchise in Charlotte, North Carolina. They had heard about my walk out from New York and wanted to know if I was prepared to discuss joining them as head coach and chief executive. Two days later a plane ticket came through my door and I was on my way to join the Carolina Lightnin'. Jean and the children followed not long after.

I had four great years at Charlotte starting in 1981. In fact, the team didn't have a name when I first went there. It was named via a competition in the local newspaper! The owner of the Lightnin' was an extremely wealthy man called Bob Benson and he was very supportive. We got on very well together. He was a terrific tennis player and we frequently played on Sunday mornings.

When I arrived, we didn't have a single player because it was the team's first year, but I quickly sorted that. In those days, an expansion side was allowed to poach one player from another team so long as he wasn't on their 12-man protected roster. That's how I built my first Lightnin' outfit. I took some players from New York as well as kit men and physios. Then I signed an ex-Tranmere Rovers lad called David Philpotts. He had been struggling with a back injury but I've rarely met anyone in the game with such enthusiasm and dedication to football. David was a dream to manage. Then I got a former Everton youth player called Don Tobin who had a terrific left foot and a great engine. He was going to be the fulcrum of my team. I scoured the country for weeks hunting for players whom I hoped would blend together. It was a collection of odds and sods from everywhere. We also had open trials. Every kid for miles who had ever pulled on a pair of football boots, and some who hadn't, tried out for the team.

Incredibly, we won the American Soccer League Division championship in our first season. At the time, there were two conferences in the ASL. The Lightnin' came top of the Freedom and, coincidentally, New York United won the Liberty. Each conference contained four teams and the standard was about that of the Nationwide Second Division.

In the first round of the playoffs we defeated the New York Eagles 4–1. Then we beat the Pennsylvania Stoners in the semi-final to set up a championship showdown with United. That game was truly one of the most amazing and exciting I've ever been involved with. It was one of the finest moments in my sporting life, too.

The championship venue was decided by the team who had the better record. New York's was superior to ours but they couldn't get a date at their Hofstra University home ground because the New York Jets baseball team had priority. So the League's commissioner ordered the game to be played in Charlotte's Memorial Stadium, which was not a problem – we were just a sleepy little town with a stadium that hardly anybody else used. United weren't at all happy but they had no option.

The drawback was there hadn't been any marketing at all in Charlotte for the game because everyone had taken it for granted that we would be in New York. So, with just 24 hours to go, our big day looked like turning into a disaster when only 2,000 tickets had been sold. This annoyed the League and CBS, the television company that had bought the rights to show the match live. They were bickering and arguing right up to the kick-off. It was farcical.

When I woke up on the morning of the game, I looked out of the window and couldn't believe it. It was raining cats and dogs. Bob Benson rang me in a panic but I told him there was nothing we could do. All day it poured, easing at about five in the evening when I was on my way to the ground to start the pre-match preparations.

When I arrived it was all doom and gloom. Then at about 6.30, with the kick-off scheduled for an hour later, hordes of people began queuing up to get into the ground. To everyone's astonishment, by 7 o'clock the stadium was engulfed by people trying to get in. We were expecting a small crowd, so just four gates had been opened. Now there was another panic to open up the rest of the turnstiles. When we kicked off 20 minutes later, it was in front of a full house. The stadium held 17,000 but there were at least 3,000 more than that in the ground. Against all the odds, Charlotte had suddenly got soccer fever. To put things into perspective, the game was probably a bit like the Autoglass Cup final – not to the people of South Carolina, though. For them, it was a big-deal championship game, which made the whole occasion brilliant.

An unstoppable 30-yard volley by one of the New York forwards which flew into the back of our net in the first half wasn't as pleasing. Nonetheless, I still felt we were in control. United probably had the better players but they didn't have our team spirit, the kind of camaraderie that helped Wimbledon beat Liverpool in the 1988 FA Cup final.

At half-time I decided to make a substitution and brought on a guy called Mal Roche. When we took the field for the second half, the atmosphere couldn't have been bettered, even in the theatre of dreams. With his first touch, Mal steered the ball to the far post of the New York goal where little Don Tobin was waiting to nod in the equaliser. When the crowd erupted, I knew it was our destiny to go on and win. The noise was decibels over anything I had heard before; or at least, that's how it felt.

In the end, it wasn't our enthusiasm that gave us victory; it was tactics. For months we had been working on corner kicks and towards the end of the game one of our set-pieces worked a treat. Tobin, who had played brilliantly, whipped over a corner from the right which was helped on to the far post by Dave Pierce, a young American defender. There, unmarked, was Hughie O'Neil, a Scots-American lad, and when he gleefully smashed the ball into the roof of the net with his head, the stadium exploded into frenzy.

I had won a championship in my first year as a coach. You might think that wasn't too great an achievement but let me tell you, the emotion I felt was equal to the sensation of playing for England and beating Scotland at Hampden Park in front of 134,000 ranting Jocks.

I'll never forget the sight of the players at a local British pub that we had booked for the celebrations. It almost brought tears to my eyes. Off their own bat, they had all hired tuxedos and black and white dicky bows. When I walked in, to a man they all stood and applauded. It was one of the happiest moments of my life.

The only thing that bothered me at the end of that smashing season was that the New York United coach, Jim McGeogh, was named coach of the year. How they worked that out I don't know. How much better can you do in your first coaching job?

It's also interesting to note that while I was cutting my managerial teeth so to speak, Malcolm Macdonald, who had lost a few of his as a battering ram of a centre-forward, had just become the Football League's first paid director at my old club, Fulham. When you think of today's game, it's amazing that it took an extraordinary general meeting of the League to get that passed. I was genuinely pleased for Malcolm. Our careers had run in a sort of parallel. Both of us had been plucked away from Craven Cottage for peanuts by Alec Stock; we had broken into the England side just months apart although he won five more caps than I did; and we had also gone into management in the same year although in different countries.

We were vastly different players. Malcolm had been converted into an old-style centre-forward after beginning his career as a left-back. Strong, brave, quick and deadly in front of goal, Macdonald was a superb goal machine for Luton, Newcastle and Arsenal. He also became the first man since the war to score five goals in an England game at Wembley. When Fulham greats are mentioned, you don't often hear about Malcolm but he was one of the finest strikers to come out of Craven Cottage, even though they didn't have the brains to give him the No. 9 shirt too often.

I always felt that Malcolm never got enough credit or praise for his ability. I found him to be forthright and opinionated and not afraid to speak his mind. I like that and when they talk about the great players of Fulham's past I hope they find a place for the bow-legged wonder.

In football management, I was still learning, not only about coaching but also marketing. That's something Americans are terrific at although they don't always get it right. One sensational promotion we had in Charlotte is a perfect example of how if anything can go wrong, it will do. Before one game I put together a stunt which we all thought would be the best in the history of American sports. I had gone to Piper, the aircraft manufacturers, the *Charlotte Observer* newspaper, TV and radio stations and some local businesses, and organised a half-time competition that had a brand-new Piper executive jet as its prize. At the time, I don't think anyone had done anything as big as that in America.

We had 50 people write their names and addresses on the back of a Frisbee and stand behind a goalline at one end of the pitch. As they did so, a magnificent blue and white twin turbo

Piper aircraft was wheeled out on to the pitch from a ramp. Then, with the TV cameras on them, the contestants hurled their Frisbees one at a time at a twin-bladed propeller standing upright in the centre circle. The closest would win the Piper jet but nobody got within 20 yards of the target until an old redneck farmer stepped forward. When he flicked his Frisbee it was like something from *Star Wars*. The disc zoomed six feet above the pitch as if guided by a laser and finally landed just inches away from the propeller.

The cheering 20,000 crowd erupted at the old guy's amazing skill. All the cameramen came running out, flashing spotlights beamed, and ticker tape was dropped all over the place. Finally, the old farmer was dragged on to the podium to collect his prize.

'What's your name?' the MC asked him, unable to conceal his own excitement.

'Charlie Farnsbarn,' came the reply.

'Well, Charlie. How does it feel? Do you know you're the first person in America to win an aircraft in a contest like this? Where in the world is your first flight going to be to?'

In front of the sponsors and live on television, Charlie irritably replied, 'I don't want it. What the hell am I going to do with a plane? I can't afford the gift tax on it. No, just take the thing away. If I'd known that was the prize, I wouldn't have bothered to enter.' And off he went leaving everyone speechless. It was the worst promotion ever seen in America.

Another promotion turned into the most hilarious sight I have ever seen in my life. This time someone on our staff came up with a half-time bag giveaway in conjunction with the US Army. As chief executive of the Lightnin', I had to approve all of these schemes and why I gave my blessing to this one I'll never know. The army said they would provide 100 beautiful leather bags for a matchday competition that would be part of a radio and TV enrolment push – join the army and win a bag, I ask you. Who in the world would dream that up? But when the top-quality leather bags turned up, I had to admit that they were superb.

During the game's half-time break, we neatly stacked them in the centre circle and asked all the children in the stadium to come down on to the pitch and line up behind one of the goals.

'OK you guys,' announced the game's MC over the PA system, 'I'm going to count down from ten. When I reach one, I'm going to say go, and the first hundred of you to get to the centre circle will win a bag. Are you ready? Ten . . .'

He didn't get any further because all the kids were off like a shot. It was one of the most comical scenes I have ever encountered, better than a Marx Brothers film. The children's mothers came running after them from the stands. They were falling over each other and punching one another, desperately trying to get to the centre circle. And when they did, it was chaos. The pitch looked more like a scene from 'Monty Python's Flying Circus' than a harmless football promotion. To top it off, the security police arrived and gave a wonderful impersonation of the Keystone Kops as they tried to separate everybody fighting for the bags. It was the last promotion we did that season.

At the beginning of 1982, the NASL started to disintegrate. Six teams had folded after the indoor season leaving just 14 to compete in the spring. There had also been an exodus of international stars including Besty, Charlie Cooke, Cruyff, Gerd Muller, Carlos Alberto and Eusebio.

That year the Lightnin' frequently had better attendances than some NASL teams. Our average gate was 8,000, the highest in the League. The conferences had been dispensed with but we couldn't quite raise our game to the standards of the previous season and were beaten in the semi-finals of the playoffs by Oklahoma.

The surge of interest didn't last and 1983 proved to be the American Soccer League's final year. For several decades before the formation of the NASL, the ASL had been the top professional league in the country. The feeling now was that the Major

Indoor Soccer League represented the future. It was all a bit sad around that time, and not only for football reasons.

During that close season something astonishing happened. One day, just before our first game, I got a phone call from Ken Adam, my old agent. Ken told me that Bobby Moore, for whom he also acted, was out of work. Ken said that the former England hero had been with a team in Hong Kong where he had been doing a bit of coaching but it had fallen through. I was stunned. I couldn't believe that an agent would have to phone around to try to fix up a job for a guy who was probably the greatest defender the game has produced. Ken asked me if I was prepared to take Bobby on as a coach at Charlotte. I didn't have to think about it.

'No problem at all,' I said. 'I'd love to have him.'

So Bobby came over and signed a six-month contract for the summer outdoor season and I gave him a good deal, which he deserved. For coming to Charlotte, Bobby got a nice salary, a house, a brand-new car and an expense account. He was absolutely brilliant. I can't speak highly enough of him. You might have thought that he would get a bit frustrated working with American kids but far from it. His patience was inexhaustible, he was always a gentleman and first class through and through.

But to start with, Bobby acted a little oddly, which surprised me. He hardly spoke, socially, that is. In training he was fine, the same old Bobby. When it was over though, he would jump into his new Camaro sportscar and I wouldn't see him until the next morning. It wasn't just me. Bobby wasn't mixing with anyone, and he hadn't once asked me out for a drink. Now, knowing him as I did, that was unusual. I didn't push it but after about 10 days, I had to ask him why. When training was over and before Bobby could shoot away again, I grabbed him.

'Bob,' I said. 'Can I have a word with you? Tell me to mind my own business but you've been over here for almost a couple of weeks and you and I haven't been out for a beer, a chat or anything. If you're waiting for me to ask, I don't think it should come from me. You're the new guy in town. I don't want to impose on you but don't you think we should go out for a beer?'

'How about tonight?' he replied.

So that evening we went to a bar and he opened up. We sat down and Bobby took a sip of his drink.

'Rod,' he said. 'I apologise. I should have told you. My girlfriend's here . . .'

Well, that completely floored me, knocked me completely off balance. I didn't know what to say. I had known Bobby and Tina, his wife, almost forever it seemed; going back to 1965 before England had won the World Cup. I knew his family, his children.

'I've kept it very quiet, Rod,' he said. 'The press haven't got hold of it. And it's the real thing. I'm going to separate from Tina and marry this girl.'

'You should have told me, Bob,' I said at last. 'It's not a big deal to me. I can keep my mouth shut.'

'I haven't told anybody at all. I don't want it to get in the press because Tina doesn't know, or the children. You know how much I love my kids.' I did know. We had been to his home many times and seen him with Roberta and Dean. He was devoted to them.

We had a big drink that night, Bobby and I; and the more we drank, the more he talked, as though he was pleased to get it off his chest at last. I just listened. He even told me what happened the night he was arrested for shoplifting in Colombia, just before the 1970 World Cup in Mexico.

The incident had begun on 18 May when a group of players including Bobby visited a jeweller's shop in the hotel where they were staying. Later, a bracelet was reported missing. The England team was allowed to leave for Ecuador after Mooro had made a statement to the police. But when the plane touched down in Bogota again *en route* for Mexico, the England captain was arrested. A witness had come forward to say that he had seen Mooro take the jewellery, which he hadn't, of course. Bobby told me he saw who did. A major international incident was averted after top-level diplomatic negotiations but not before Bobby had been detained for two days. Even so, he never grassed on the real culprit and that's so typical of the man and another indication of how great he was. Most people think Bobby died without disclosing who took the bracelet. I don't know if he told anyone else other than me, but I'm definitely not saying who it was.

The day after our drinking session, Bobby introduced me to his future wife, Stephanie, at a squash club where we all had membership as part of our contracts. The rest, as they say, is history. The following week Stephanie, who was an air hostess at the time and a lovely lady, had to go back to work and pick up a flight to the Middle East. A few days after that, Tina arrived to join Bobby with their two children and I guess what happened next was a bit predictable. Later Bobby told me what occurred.

Tina hadn't been there long when the postman delivered the phone bill. Bobby was training and so Tina opened it. Listed were calls to and from locations all over the world, a log of how Bobby and Stephanie had been keeping in touch. Of course, when Bobby got back, Tina wanted to know why Bobby had been making so many international calls. He didn't prolong the agony and admitted to the infidelity there and then. Tina was obviously devastated.

The next night I had an early season party for the football club at our home, which was situated on a hill overlooking a gorgeous valley. Jean had gone to England to visit her mother and I had invited about 150 people, including Bobby and Tina. During the evening most of us had congregated on the wrap-around balcony, drinking, chatting and admiring the view. Tina was at one end and I was with Bobby at the other. They were probably about 40 feet apart. Bobby hadn't told me about his confession to Tina but you could tell there was incredible friction between them. It was that night that she announced she was divorcing him.

Stephanie returned several times during that summer and she handled everything with great dignity. Eventually, as we all know, Bobby and Stephanie were married. It was one of life's saddest stories when he passed away just over a decade later.

In October 1983, I got a call from Dick Corbett, one of the new owners of the Tampa Bay Rowdies. Dick asked me if I would like to return to Tampa as head coach and chief executive. I told him that I would only do the job on the same terms as my previous clubs and that involved autonomy over all the players. Nobody would come or go without my permission. It is the only way to run a football club properly. Dick didn't hesitate and immediately agreed. It was a great opportunity to get the family back to Florida.

Dick and his wife Cornelia, who was to have a big role with the Rowdies, had moved to Tampa in 1978. They were a mad sports couple who had met on the ski slopes. Dick had been a former lightweight amateur boxer and he had a nose that had been broken in six places to prove it. Even their vacations were taken playing golf, white water rafting in Colorado or climbing in the Grand Canyon. They are a great couple and I took to them from the start. My role was to run the football side of the Rowdies and Cornelia would be in charge of everything else as Dick's business interests increased.

Born in Manhattan in 1946, Cornelia was from a very well-to-do family. Her father was in investments and her mother owned racehorses. Her grandfather was Averell Harriman, the famous American financier and diplomat, and his father founded the Union Pacific railroad. Cornelia had a private income. They were a wild couple when they met in 1968, and their honeymoon was spent on a three-month hike through Nepal and the Himalayas often sleeping in mud huts. After living in luxury in New York that must have been something! They were my kind of people.

But 1984 was the final season of the NASL. Attendances had been on a downward spiral for some years and although there were crowds of over 100,000 for that summer's Olympic soccer games, most NASL league sides couldn't even manage 10,000. What a far cry that was from my halcyon days as an NASL player.

The biggest attendance of the season was for a Minnesota Strikers match. It drew more than 50,000 – but that was only because the Beach Boys performed after the game. Things became so desperate for the Cosmos that they asked Pele to return, seven years after his final season. Fortunately, the great man had the good grace to say no. After that, they continued purely as an exhibition side, like the Harlem Globetrotters.

Among the ashes of American soccer, I discovered a player who could, and should, have set the football world alight. One day I was sitting in the stands by myself watching the University of Florida. They had an 18-year-old South African boy on the wing and I had not seen a player in America at that age with the same talent and speed. He was clearly far superior to any other footballer around at the time. I couldn't keep my eyes off him as he outran people with and without the ball. His name was Roy Wegerle. I already knew his brother Steve, so after the game I asked Roy to drop out of school and join the Rowdies. He agreed and we gave him a terrific package that included a good salary and a college education if he wanted to go back to school.

The first season Roy played for the Rowdies was astonishing. He did things to defences that weren't believable for a boy that young. I played him straightaway and he ended up scoring 15 goals in 12 games. He was so good that when the year finished I didn't feel it was right to hold him back. I thought he should be playing in England's First Division and he agreed.

So I phoned Malcolm Allison and asked who would take him. Malcolm suggested Chelsea, which led to Roy going to Stamford Bridge on loan. He was so breathtaking in his first two games for the reserves that the Blues decided to sign him there and then.

Chelsea eventually let him go and he played for Luton, QPR,

Blackburn and Coventry, but in my opinion he wasn't looked after properly. He was such a gifted lad. In fact, he never played in the UK like he played for me in Tampa. With a little bit of sympathetic handling, I believe Roy could have been a truly great player.

My first season in charge at the Rowdies wasn't too great and I'm the first to admit it. Tampa won nine out of 12 home games but we finished bottom of the last NASL Eastern Division because we lost all our away games. We just couldn't travel. I know precisely what George Graham went through at Spurs before he was fired.

After the League folded, we ran a very successful summer coaching programme called Kamp Kick in the Grass, which was started by the referee Gordon Hill. This was a training scheme for kids, day and residential, and it was something in which the whole Rowdies team participated. On a rotation basis, the players coached the youngsters over a 13-week summer period. At one stage we were getting as many as 2,000 children for the course.

In 1986, the Rowdies invited Queens Park Rangers over for a set of exhibition games, which they played under the name of the Queens Park Rowdies. Jim Smith was in charge at Loftus Road at the time and his number two was Frank Sibley, who had become Rangers' youngest ever player, aged 16.

Jim and Frank are smashing people and the whole trip was a pleasure. My daughter Joanna had a teenage crush on Justin Channing, Rangers' young left-back. It all went wrong when one of the players and a few of his mates smashed up a bar and a girl's apartment. The police were called and the damage they caused came to thousands of dollars. The Rowdies had to cough up to get them out of jail.

The really special moment of that year was an anniversary game between the old players of the Rowdies glory years and the US national team in Tampa Stadium. What a terrific night it was for the 25,000 spectators because we had managed to persuade

Spurs superstars Glenn Hoddle and Ossie Ardiles to guest for the Rowdies. I was 42 years old but I came on as a second-half substitute for the last 20 minutes. The score at the time was 2–2 and Glenn had put on an absolutely brilliant performance. I'd not been on the pitch long when Hoddle controlled a pass on the right of the halfway line. As he did, I caught his eye from the edge of the penalty box. Spinning off my marker, I dashed into the box to collect an inch-perfect gem of a pass from Glenn which was precision itself with perfect height and weight. Glenn had also anticipated that, at my age, I was two or three yards slower than I once was, and the ball came down on to my foot like a feather. At that moment I realised just what a great footballer Glenn Hoddle was.

The following year the Rowdies joined the American Indoor Soccer Association and then the American Soccer League, which was really a minor league. By then I had relinquished my coaching duties to concentrate on the job of chief executive. I had also become a close personal friend of both Cornelia and Dick Corbett.

It was my job to hire coaches for the club. The first was Mark Lawrenson, the former Liverpool defender who came over from England in the capacity of player-coach. I can't speak highly enough of Mark and his abilities. He is a complete professional and it's a mystery to me why he isn't running a Premiership club.

Mark was with us for a year before going back to the UK. I invited Malcolm Allison to fill the vacancy. Despite what Jean says, at the time I still had a soft spot for him but after he arrived I realised that Malcolm had completely lost the plot in terms of his coaching. When I first met him in 1972 at Manchester City, he was one of the greatest coaches that I had ever been around, so far ahead of his time and so progressive. His techniques and tactics and the way he approached his job were second to none. Yet when he came to work for me in 1988, he'd gone radical about coaching. Here are a couple of examples that just about sum him up at the time.

After a game one night we went to the post-match party at a local restaurant. This is a kind of a ritual in American sport, a tradition. It gives the fans an opportunity to come face to face with the manager and the players, which is great PR. After it was over, I went home with my family leaving Malcolm to it. At about 3.30 in the morning the phone rang. When I picked it up a policeman told me a man they had in the cells had given my name as a reference. I asked what had happened and the cop said that the guy's name was Malcolm Allison and he had been arrested driving at eight miles an hour on the wrong side of the road over the Courtney Campbell Causeway, a seven-mile bridge that spans Tampa Bay, completely drunk. He asked if I would come to the police station and stand bail.

'No,' I replied. 'Leave him there. We'll do it in the morning.' Then I put the phone down. The next day, I sent one of our trainers to get him out but Malcolm had now reached the last chance saloon.

In spite of everything, like his drinking and eccentric behaviour, I still spoke very highly of Malcolm – God knows why – even to Cornelia Corbett, who was on the US national team committee. I put his name forward for the then vacant position of coach to the American national side. Malcolm seemed really pleased when I told him but he had to meet with Cornelia and outline his plan, if he had one, for how he would get the United States up there with the Brazils of the world. Malcolm said he did indeed have a plan to achieve this and we arranged to meet Cornelia for dinner in Tampa.

I picked her up and when we got to the restaurant Malcolm was already resplendent – Dom Perignon in the ice bucket, empty of course, and clearly the worse for wear. Even so, I felt we had to go through with the interview because it really was Malcolm's last chance. So after the introductions we sat down and joined Malcolm in a glass of champagne. Cornelia accepted the situation in the best possible way. She was prepared to listen to Malcolm, in spite of the condition he was in.

'Malcolm,' Cornelia asked, 'could you tell me your plans for American soccer?'

'Well,' said Malcolm with a serious look on his face, 'you've got so many big people in this country that I would only have players six feet six inches tall and above in the side. And because of that, all of our tactics would be in the air . . .'

'Christ,' I shouted to myself, in my head. It was patently obvious that Malcolm was out of it.

I looked nervously towards Cornelia but she just tilted her head in the air and rolled her eyes. Malcolm launched into one of his diatribes, which was liberally sprinkled with effs and blinds, on how no one understood him and why he was the only person in the world who could lead the United States forward. Cornelia sat there patiently finishing her drink. Then she convivially thanked Malcolm for his time and bade him farewell. That was the last America saw of Malcolm Allison.

During that time, we signed some good players, including former England internationals Peter Ward and Peter Barnes, and ex-Chelsea defender Steve Wicks. Then there was Tommy 'Disney World' Langley. Tommy acquired his nickname during a very short spell with us that quickly landed him in hot water. When British players came to Tampa I used to tell them that I understood they were in Florida for the summer and it was OK to have some good times because there would be plenty of days off, but football must always come first.

The Thursday before a Saturday game in Tampa Stadium, Tommy didn't turn up for training. There was no message or word and, despite my efforts to track him down, he was nowhere to be found. He was missing again the following day. Eventually, someone telephoned to tell me that he had taken his family to Disney World for two days and would meet up with the team before the game. He thought that wouldn't be a problem. Yeah, right!

Tommy had been playing well so I decided to start with him anyway but not before I had given him a kick up the backside. He immediately held up his hands and said he was out of order. I fined him a week's wages, just to get my point across.

Worse than that was to follow for Tommy because in the first five minutes, as he was going down the wing, he pulled up with a ruptured hamstring. That was down to him not stretching or doing any exercises before the match. The following day, after he had received treatment, I called him into the office and gave him an airline ticket.

'OK, Disney World,' I told him. 'Now you can fuck off home.'

The injury had put him out for two months and it was all his own doing, so why should the club be responsible for paying his wages?

The next coach I got after Malcolm was Luton's Ricky Hill and he did quite well but I didn't think he was hard enough to be a manager. He is a very nice guy, a Ray Wilkins type. Somehow, I didn't feel he possessed the cutting edge to make it at that level.

After Ricky came David Hay, the former Celtic, Chelsea and Scotland star, but his family couldn't settle in the States and so he didn't stay long. David was followed by Ken Fogarty, a former Everton player, and he coached the Rowdies until America completely lost its way in soccer in 1993. The crowds were down to a mere 700 or 800 people by that time.

Cornelia lost a staggering $9 million on the Rowdies. She wanted to continue but I told her, 'No, it's never going to work in this country. Enough is enough.'

That year, the whole League folded and there was no organised soccer in the United States. Nevertheless, the next year America hosted the World Cup, which turned out to be the most successful ever.

Cornelia and I had sat on the original committee that put together America's World Cup application. One of our tasks was to raise $75,000 to pay for the first investors' information brochure. We did that quite easily and in return for our efforts and our expertise we were given a promise that one of the tournament's venues would be Tampa. At the eleventh hour, Alan Rothenberg, who was the chairman of World Cup USA 1994, together with the site committee, chose Orlando instead. Cornelia took this personally. Tampa clearly had better facilities, a soccer history, good hotels and travel infrastructure. The only things Orlando had in its favour were Disney and the fact that the McDonald's fast-food chain wanted it there. The place had never had a team of note and had no soccer history. It seemed to us that the decision had nothing whatsoever to do with the game and everything to do with big business wanting to make money. To say that Tampa wouldn't have been a fitting stage is nothing short of ridiculous because the city has staged three NFL SuperBowls.

Today, Major League Soccer in America is not working. I want football to be popular in the States again because I have many wonderful memories of my time there and I still part own the Tampa Bay Rowdies franchise. The problem is that the Americans don't understand football's fundamental need – tradition. Football needs a dynasty to survive and that is what they don't have at the moment.

Major League Soccer started in 1996 with the backing of six major sponsors. It is a single entity. The MLS franchise the teams to investors. They own all the players' contracts and decide who plays for which team. There are no transfers but trades are allowed. There has been speculation that some teams may move to new cities, like they do in other sports in the States. For instance, in the near future the Tampa Bay Mutiny might go to New Orleans and the Miami Fusion could go to the New York area.

There is also a salary cap of approximately $240,000 per player (around £170,000) per year. Teams can get around this with sponsorship deals and top players such as Los Angeles

Aztecs' Cobi Jones and German star Lothar Matthaus, who played for the New York/New Jersey MetroStars, can bank a million dollars a year. Paul Gascoigne has said that he would like to finish his career in the States and Gazza will certainly top that figure if he does go there.

When I was playing in the original North American Soccer League, it was a massive success because the best players in the world were there. Every city had a major superstar, and soccer was on the biggest mainstream channel, ABC. Allegedly, that was something the baseball league and the National Football League weren't happy about and it is said they threatened to go elsewhere if the TV channels didn't stop showing soccer. I don't know if that's true or not but after a while I can only remember games being shown on regional TV, except for the MLS championship and certain internationals. Gradually, the genuine superstars were replaced with mediocre foreign players of whom no one had heard. For those reasons, crowds dipped dramatically and soccer in the US has never recovered.

The US national team has come on in leaps and bounds, though. I guess that was inevitable in a country with so many great athletes. The US is very close to becoming a decent international team. In the last few years, they have lost narrowly to Brazil 2–1 and they have beaten Mexico 2–0. They have also won against Germany and Portugal.

I had a fantastic time in America. I don't think I ever enjoyed my football as much as when I was playing for Tampa Bay Rowdies. There was colour, flair, wonderful pitches and stadiums, plus incredible crowds. I have a million fond memories. One of my fondest, at least from a playing point of view, is of the time I met up with Rildo, Brazil's left-back in the 1966 World Cup. We had played against each other a few times and after I had retired from playing, I bumped into him at a football dinner. He was coaching a minor team in California. During the evening he said that he remembered me very well from the days when he played for the New York Cosmos and I was with the Rowdies.

'Rodney,' he said, 'I first heard of you before one match we had against each other in the Giants' Stadium. I can remember the crowd calling your name even though Pele was playing for us. Our team manager was giving his team-talk before the game, which was useful to me because I had just come from Brazil and didn't know anything about the opposition.'

Rildo told me that when the coach had finished, Pele got to his feet, asked everybody to be quiet and said, 'Tampa are a good team. They have one player in particular to watch out for. His name is Rodney Marsh. He wears the No. 10. He's English but he plays like a Brazilian.'

That's the nicest compliment anyone has paid me. It doesn't actually make a difference whether it was Pele who said it or Joe Soap. I've always considered myself a Brazilian-style player and I would have loved to play there.

I'm confident the Americans will find the continuity they need. There's a massive youth system in place, lots of academies and millions of youngsters playing the game. In a country of 260 million people the future looks very strong, and when they get it right the rest of the world had better look out.

After the demise of the Rowdies in 1993, I was sitting by the swimming pool one day, wondering what direction my life might take, when I got a telephone call about yet another link-up with George. This time I had a cup of tea in my hand but it was good enough to toast a comeback with him. We might have been well past it on a football pitch, but I knew the two of us were still capable of producing some magic.

get the show on the road, mary

If they liked you they didn't applaud – they just let you live!

Bob Hope

Mary Shatali introduced herself to me on the telephone as George Best's live-in girlfriend and partner. We had never spoken before so it did cross my mind to ask if she could prove it; but as Mary had been brave enough to admit it in the first place, I guess that was good enough. Such was George's reputation when he met her in 1987.

George isn't one of the most organised blokes in the world, as he will agree, and that was the main reason he was in such deep water with the Inland Revenue in the late 1980s. Besty had never tried to avoid paying tax; he was just unable to keep track or account of his personal appearances. Blondes seemed to bring out the worst in him; it took a brunette to help him just when he needed it the most.

After George and Mary had become acquainted in Blondes nightspot, Mary's sister told her not to touch Besty with a barge pole. It was lucky for George that she chose to ignore that advice for it was Mary who motivated his rescue from the sea of debt he was in at the time. From then on, she so skilfully managed Besty's life that within a few years he was back in shape businesswise, and eventually out of trouble with the tax authorities.

Besty was certainly not coy in some respects, as everyone knows, but in those days he could be painfully shy in public and through Mary's encouragement, George managed to shed this affliction and launch a new career on the lucrative after-dinner speaking circuit. That was the reason for her call to me in Florida. Without each other's knowledge, George and I had been independently hired to speak at a function in Manchester. When Mary discovered we would be sharing the same bill, she contacted me to ask how I wanted to approach the evening.

I hadn't seen George for a few years and when we met in Manchester before the event, it was just like old times. We'd always been friends and it was just like meeting up with a long-lost brother. The dinner was terrific – full of old City and United players talking about football. After the meal, George got up and delivered an hilarious speech. When he had finished I followed by telling everybody that I wasn't going to compete but I would answer any questions from the floor.

George and I went backwards and forwards for an hour longer than we should have. We were laughing, joking and giving everyone great crack. All the old football stories came flooding back and it was just one brilliant night. When it was over, we got a standing ovation which seemed to last for ages. It was fantastic.

Later, over a few glasses of champagne in the Midland Hotel, Mary asked George and I if we fancied doing a series of similar events. We did a quick double take and then agreed we were up for it although I thought what we really needed was a sponsor and somebody to promote the tour. Within six weeks, Mary had both and a bunch of dates, too. That was the start of the Best and Marsh Roadshow.

Some people thought a tour like that would be a complete disaster, especially with George's reputation. But we did a lot of hugely successful shows that were so enjoyable for everybody concerned. It gave me almost as much pleasure to prove a lot of those sceptics wrong.

Lord Snowdon, Anthony Armstrong Jones, took this picture of me for a feature in the *Sunday Times* in 1968 when I was still playing for QPR. (*Lord Snowdon*)

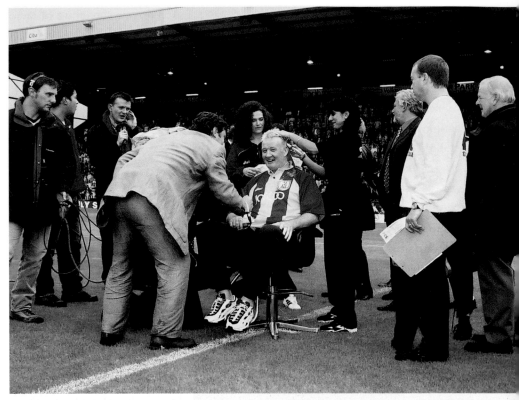

The Bradford head shave. The first cut is made as Sky reporter Ned Boulting gets my reaction in front of a full house at Valley Parade. (*Melissa Chappell*)

Soccer Saturday presenter Jeff Stelling receives my congratulations after winning the 2001 Best Sports Presenter Award.

Over the years people have built up an image of George as irresponsible, unreliable and a waster who at times just doesn't care. All that is on his mind, they believe, is drinking, sex and gambling, and not necessarily in that order. People reckon George's life is made up only of those things. There might have been an element of truth in that at one time, but during the roadshow the most excitement we got together was doing a tabloid crossword. When people used to see us get in our limousine to go to different gigs, they'd think it was full of champagne, women and porno films, but it was not so. When we travelled from show to show, it was usually just the two of us. Mary might join us on some nights but no one else. We always had a bottle of white wine in the back of the limo and sometimes the only conversation we had was when George asked something like, 'Marshy? Fourteen across. German river beginning with the letter R?'

In Joe Lovejoy's authorised biography, George is quoted as saying, 'Doing the London Palladium was the highlight. What a night that was! People don't realise what hard work it is. The actual show is the easy part. It's what goes with it. The hours of travelling between venues, the endless handshaking, the chatting, the photographs. There may be eight hundred people there, and at the end of the show you might have to sit there for another two hours to satisfy them. It's part of the job.'

So all those people who thought the Best and Marsh Roadshow was all sex, fun and rock 'n' roll were completely wrong; it never happened.

All in all, we probably did between three and four hundred dates over a three-year period. In the end, the travelling got us down. I was still based in America and would come over to the UK for a month and do maybe 20 shows in 30 days. It was hard work but nonetheless great crack.

We did slip up on the odd occasion, of course. If I had been allowed to manage those situations, everything would have been all right on the night. The thing about Besty, and it's not his fault at all, is that a lot of people go to pieces in his company, which can lead to disastrous consequences. I've seen superstars open-mouthed and heard them asking stupid childish questions merely to talk to him. He has that effect on people.

One day we were booked to do two shows in one day in Manchester. One was a lunch for over a thousand people at the Piccadilly Hotel and the other was a dinner in the evening at the Mere Golf and Country Club. The lunch went very well. George was in great form. It seems like it was only yesterday. He was as sharp as a tack with any questions and we got a standing ovation. Everyone was well pleased.

Afterwards we went to the Midland Hotel where we always stayed when we were in the area because George was a great friend of Sean McCarthy, the chief executive. George asked me if I wanted a quick glass of champagne but I declined because I wanted a nap and a shower. We arranged to meet in the bar at 6.00 p.m.

When I got downstairs at the appointed time, the red flag went up because George hadn't moved from where I had left him a couple of hours earlier. He had clearly had a few drinks and to make things even worse, he had been suffering with a bout of 'flu for a couple of days.

Not long afterwards the promoter arrived and we eventually coaxed George upstairs where he showered and dressed for the extremely elegant black tie do. When we got to the Mere, it was a toss up whether George could do the show or not. But as soon as we arrived, someone put a glass of champagne into George's hand; and he insisted on plying George with more and more bubbly, glass after glass. What a prat! 'Here we go,' I thought. 'This is definitely going to be a problem now.'

I'd seen it before but every time it happens I'm stunned. Intelligent grown men become quivering wrecks in front of George. His aura overpowers them and they completely lose perspective and act like little children. I mean, when someone is so obviously drunk, as George was then, you don't give them more, do you? That's plain stupidity. Yet some people don't seem able to help themselves. That night George had gone past the point of no return but still there were people forcing the stuff on him. These people are arseholes. When it all goes wrong, they blame George, and that's exactly what happened this time.

Neil Midgley, the old official who once famously said he only took up refereeing when his eyesight began to fade, was the Master of Ceremonies. I seemed to be the only one who could see what was likely to happen in the next 90 minutes. Perhaps that's because I hadn't been drinking.

'Neil,' I said, 'I think we're going to have to get George on pretty sharpish tonight. Why don't we change the whole thing around and we'll give our speech before dinner?'

'Oh, I'm not sure we can do that,' he replied.

'Well, if you don't, it's all going to be off,' I told him.

Neil called the sponsor over and explained what I wanted to do.

'No,' he said. 'We'll carry on as normal.'

I just shook my head. When more drink was forced in George's direction I knew I had to keep my eye on him. He had hit the wall, the point where even he couldn't drink any more, and when that happens, expect George to do a runner. But he didn't; he just sat there. The soup was served and I heard a wallop as George fell forward and his head landed in the bowl. The plate lay smashed on the table and there was tomato soup all over his beard, hair and tuxedo. We carried him to the toilets and cleaned him up before bringing him back to the top table. Everybody started to boo. It was so sad. I took the microphone from Neil.

'Ladies and gentlemen,' I said. 'George has had a long day today, and he's not well. But in an effort to appease you all, perhaps you would like to ask him a few questions and I'll say a few words after?'

This was greeted with even more derisory comments. People started shouting that it was all a rip-off and when it became really nasty I announced that we couldn't continue, apologised and helped George, who was out of it, to the hotel reception area. When we got there the pandemonium was still going on so I thought it best if we left as soon as we could. I also wanted to get George away because I thought he was going to be very, very ill.

Eventually, Mary and I laid him on the back seat of our limo and as we drove out through the Mere's gates, George pulled himself up on one elbow and said, 'Hey, Marshy. Did you get the readies?'

'You're having a laugh,' I said. 'We've just been chucked out!'

That was the only incident like that I can remember. To balance the books, here's another story. It's one you'll never read in the newspapers because the media are so obsessed with just one side of George.

A school in Hampshire had written to Sky's 'Soccer Saturday' with a request for George and I to give out the awards at their Under-14s prize-giving day. It was also the day of one of our shows in Bournemouth, so we agreed. There was no payment involved and neither of us thought of asking for one because we both believe there are times when you have to give back. We always tried to fit in as many of these events as we could.

When we got to the school we met the headmaster and all concerned and George gave out the prizes. In all, there were probably about 400 kids there. Afterwards, the local press wanted a picture of us heading footballs with the children and we were happy to oblige. They were all such smashing people that we stayed for a couple of hours longer than we had planned, playing head tennis and generally knocking the ball around with the kids. They loved it and you could see how much George enjoyed it, too. It's great watching him do things like that.

Eventually, we had to leave for our date on the coast and they clapped us out as we left. It was brilliant. About 10 minutes later on the motorway, George said to me, 'Hey, Marshy, look at this.' He pulled up his tracksuit leggings and his knee had doubled in size. It was just a puffy mass of fluid and giving George a lot of pain.

Now, that's the sort of thing you never hear about. George has done things like that on countless occasions but all you ever hear are the negative stories, the falling down drunk in the gutter stuff that some of the tabloids love. It's about time that was put right.

George and I made a few videos at the time. The first was about the roadshow; the second was 'Drugs, Mugs and Thugs'. This tape took a look at the game after Lee Bowyer and Dean Chandler, then both with Charlton, had been charged by the FA for drug-related offences; Eric Cantona's assault on a Crystal Palace spectator; and the match-fixing allegations surrounding Bruce Grobbelaar. The last video we did was with football agent Eric Hall and it was so bad it will probably haunt me for the rest of my life!

Slowly but surely my television career began to take off. Earlier in the decade, I had appeared in a few fill-in spots on BSkyB's 'Sports Saturday' with Sue Barker and Paul Dempsey. After that, I had made my debut on 'Soccer Saturday' alongside Mark Lawrenson and Alan Brazil.

The Best and Marsh Roadshow continued on the club circuit for the next two years, but it was a solo performance by me that started a merry-go-round of London football club managers towards the end of 1994.

CHAPTER 10

in to save qpr

I know him well. He's a bit of a shady character. Me.

Gerry Francis announcing his return to
QPR as Director of Football, 1998

One morning in October 1994, I got a phone call at my flat in
Wimbledon. I was just about to get into the bath, which was
fitting really because a few people would be in hot water as a
consequence of the conversation I was about to have.

The call was from Richard Thompson, who with his father
David then owned QPR. They are members of one of Britain's
wealthiest families, and reportedly worth in excess of £400
million. Thompson senior, a racehorse owner, made his money
from the Hillsdown food and property group. They later bought a
significant interest in Leeds Sporting, the company that owns
Leeds United and Sports Internet, which was sold to BSkyB last
year for £250 million.

Rangers had finished fifth in the Premier League's inaugural
season but, 18 months later, I could see that if they didn't stop
making such dreadful errors, they were for the drop. That's
exactly what happened in 1996 when Rangers were relegated
with Manchester City and Bolton Wanderers. Given the chance,
I'm sure I could have prevented that from happening.

'Rodney,' said the voice on the end of the line. 'It's Richard

Thompson. I'd like to have a word with you. I think there is something that you might be able to help me with.'

'Richard,' I said, 'it's fascinating that you have called me, because I was just about to contact you.'

'Why?' Thompson replied.

'Well,' I said. 'I'll tell you when I see you.'

We arranged to meet at his office in Dover Street, near London's Piccadilly. It was very palatial indeed. When we met, Richard asked me to tell him what was on my mind first. So, never being one to hold back, I let him have it.

'You are making a lot of mistakes at Rangers at the moment,' I said, 'and I was going to call you to let you know that I'm available if you would like me to consult. I can see exactly where you are going wrong. Right now all you are doing is pissing off the supporters. In fact, you're pissing off everybody.'

At the time, Gerry Francis was the manager at Loftus Road. He seemed to me to be criticising Rangers' lack of ambition too often and publicly threatening to leave because the club wanted to sell its top players. He was right but those sort of things should never be discussed publicly. A similar situation led to George Graham's downfall as the Spurs manager. Francis had even said he wasn't worried about things at Rangers because he was a wealthy man, had other business interests and didn't need football. I think that is precisely the sort of comment that could get up the noses of true blue-and-white QPR supporters.

I told Richard what was going on at QPR at the time was ridiculous and I said I couldn't understand why he hadn't given any response, or done anything for that matter.

'That's exactly what I want to talk to you about,' he said. 'How do you see QPR football club and what is your opinion on how it's being run? Because Gerry and I have an enormous problem.'

Again, I came straight to the point. I told Richard some of the recent mistakes had been nothing short of shocking. For a start,

Gerry had been allowed to speak to Wolverhampton Wanderers about their job but when the Molineux board agreed to everything Francis wanted, he turned them down.

'When Gerry returned,' I continued, 'you offered him a new improved deal. From my point of view, that was a big mistake. You can't allow people to hold you to ransom. What must the supporters be thinking? The whole situation makes you look a complete prat. That's why they protest against you outside the ground. You need to make a statement about the club. Be honest and stick to it. That's all *genuine* supporters want!'

'That's precisely why I want you on board,' he told me. 'I want you to be in between me, the board and Gerry.'

I asked him exactly how he saw my role. His reply was that I would be chief executive of Rangers. The salary would be £150,000 a year basic, plus a percentage of the gross revenue and a range of other incentives and perks. I asked Richard to be more precise about what I would actually be responsible for.

'I want you to run the football club,' he said. 'Whether or not you see the manager as being the right person for the job is for you to decide, as will be the direction of the club. To put it simply, I want you to run the club.'

I thanked Richard for his time and the offer and asked for 24 hours to think about it. The more I thought, the better I liked it. It wasn't a new situation for me really, because I'd had a similar job with the Tampa Bay Rowdies and been quite successful. So the next day I telephoned Richard and said that I was interested but there were a few things I would like clarified before I could accept the position. So we arranged to meet at his office in the afternoon.

When I got there, I told Richard my first proviso was that I had to have complete *carte blanche* over the playing staff and it would have to be me, in consultation with the manager, who decided who of the players went and who stayed.

'This is my point,' I said. 'Les Ferdinand is currently Rangers' best player and there has been a lot of speculation about his future with reports that several clubs have made five million pound bids for him. [Eight months later he was, in fact, sold to Newcastle for £6 million to replace Andy Cole who had moved to Manchester United.] Now, I can understand how tempting an offer like that can be but if you let your best players leave, the club will go down the toilet. On the other hand, I can also appreciate that there are situations in which the club is forced to raise money, and as chief executive I would want to share that responsibility.

'For all that, if the club needs capital, the board should first inform me. Then I would go to the team manager, whoever it may be, and ask for his opinion because he is the man responsible for the team's performances on the pitch. I would make it clear the club had to make some money and ask would he prefer someone like Les to be sold or can we do something else with other players?

'You can't hold a shotgun to the team manager's head and tell him, "Look, mate, we're selling so and so and you haven't got a say in the matter." You can't hold him responsible for results and flog his best players at the same time.'

Richard listened intently but said my request was something he had to think about.

My second proviso was that I should be allowed to speak to Gerry Francis before formally taking over. If Gerry wasn't going to be happy with his role, I would have to know before going in. Curiously, Thompson asked if he could come back to me on that, too. I didn't know why and he didn't offer an explanation. I suggested we talk again the following day.

The next afternoon I was back and this time he had his father David holding on a conference call. We had what's described in politics as a frank and meaningful discussion over my two conditions. When we had finished David Thompson said, 'We don't have a problem with your second request about speaking to

Francis, but there is a real issue on your first point. Supposing you don't want to sell a player and we think he should go?'

'Well, that's the whole crux of the matter,' I told him. 'You can't let your best players go. You have to find other ways around the situation. It's as simple as that.'

'OK, Rodney,' David Thompson replied. 'You've got a deal.'

So I shook hands with Richard and asked him to draw up the papers.

'Done,' he said.

I sensed there were more problems than you normally get between manager and chairman. Thompson was a refined public schoolboy type who disliked confrontation and it seemed he was having problems dealing with Gerry Francis, who is a typical hard-nosed football man. Thompson clearly found this difficult and my role really was to troubleshoot at QPR.

We left it that over the weekend he would think how we were going to announce the appointment. I suggested that it might be an idea to meet with Gerry sometime during the night of Rangers' next home game, against Liverpool on the following Monday, and hold a press conference afterwards.

Over the weekend the *Sun* newspaper got hold of the story, which to this day confuses me because I thought the only three people who knew about the deal were Richard and David Thompson and me. The morning of the fixture against the Merseysiders, my appointment was the *Sun*'s back-page lead in a story headlined 'Rod In To Save QPR'. So when I arrived at Loftus Road that evening, everybody and his dog were there, including the press and television cameras. I watched the game, which Rangers won 2–1 thanks to goals by Trevor Sinclair and Ferdinand, from the directors' box with Terry Venables. It was a memorable victory over a good Liverpool outfit. They finished in fourth place in the Premiership that season.

Gerry showed his displeasure by not attending the after-match press conference. Instead, he stormed upstairs to see

Richard Thompson and went ballistic.

'What the fucking hell are you doing?' he said. 'You've gone behind my back with Rodney Marsh. You've made it all look like a Disney World promotion.'

Peter Ellis, the chairman of the club at the time, hadn't been informed either, which was why he denied any knowledge of my position when approached by Francis during the day.

Gerry resigned after the following Saturday's clash with Newcastle. After a furious meeting with Thompson, Gerry said, 'It did not matter if the club's offer was to Donald Duck or Rodney Marsh. The fact is that I knew nothing about the situation at all. That was the straw that broke the camel's back. I had a lot of talks with a lot of people and still felt I had to hand in my resignation.

'You have to live by certain principles in life and that's what I have got. I just hope that QPR do not suffer and that my career in football will not suffer either.'

Less than two weeks later, Francis was appointed Tottenham's manager after Ossie Ardiles had been sacked, taking coaches Roger Cross and Des Bulpin with him. Ray Wilkins became manager of Rangers, initially assisted by Frank Stapleton. Former West Ham boss Billy Bonds joined them as youth-team coach. Amazing repercussions, when you think about it.

Nonetheless, I was the chief executive of QPR and I was going to do what I was going to do no matter what. Then I got another phone call asking me to attend yet another meeting in Richard Thompson's central London office. On telephone conference call, David Thompson said, 'Rodney, we've got a problem. Peter Ellis doesn't think you're right for the job.'

'Why's that?' I asked.

'Because he thinks you're a big-time champagne Charlie and he says you embezzled money from Rangers when you were a player.'

How about that then! Footballers are frequently accused of

many things but I've never heard of one having his fingers in the till, have you? How ridiculous can you get? Players don't get near the books let alone have the opportunity to practise some creative accounting. Within hours, Ellis was in receipt of a registered letter from my solicitor advising him of the certainty of legal action if in fact he had made those remarks. Twenty-four hours later came Ellis's reply in which he categorically denied the statements attributed to him by Thompson, and he apologised profusely for any offence he may have caused to me or my family.

Then David Thompson said he had a problem with the amount of money Rangers had agreed to pay me. He thought it was far too much.

'Wait a minute,' I said. 'Last week during our conference call, you agreed to that salary and Richard and I shook hands on the deal.' Richard confirmed it. David Thompson explained how he saw the situation.

'Peter Ellis as the chairman doesn't want you,' he said, 'but you've agreed and shaken hands on the deal. On top of that, we won't give you sole approval on which players can come and go. So the choice is yours. You can stay under these circumstances or you can take a substantial amount of money and go quietly.' I didn't have to think twice.

'That'll do for me, pal,' I replied.

At the time, I said publicly, 'Richard Thompson has told me he has withdrawn his offer in the best interests of Queens Park Rangers. I have a lot of respect for him and admire him for making a decision which he believes to be totally in the club's interest. A club's needs must always come before an individual. I would have appreciated the opportunity to sit down with Gerry and talk things through but it was not to be.

'I want to wish Rangers and their fans every success and hope they can put this week behind them and get on with what's important and that's getting results on the pitch. From my meetings with Richard Thompson, I would say that he is QPR through and through. Richard felt the decision was the best thing for the club and who am I to argue with that. I'll be there in the future, the blue-and-white scarf wrapped around my neck.'

Privately, I felt I had been thoroughly used but I wasn't bitter then and I'm not now. I was well paid for my trouble. Now I know how prostitutes feel. This is how I see it. Rangers didn't want to sack Francis but they wanted shot of him, so they manufactured a situation that they knew would force him to resign, and it worked. I don't know that, but if it's true I've got to hold my hands up, because it was brilliant!

I don't think I've ever said a bad word against Gerry although I thought he used Wolves to get a better deal at Rangers. But that was his choice and who am I to criticise? I've already mentioned what he was like when he broke into that fabulous Rangers side when I was in my prime and he was a tremendously talented boy.

CHAPTER 11

the man for all seasons

*A lot of people seem to think that I'm a slippery Cockney boy
with a few jokes. It has taken one of the biggest clubs in the
world to acknowledge what I can really do . . . coach!*

Terry Venables, Barcelona manager, 1985

I haven't encountered many people as naturally talented as Terry
Venables. From the first time we met, I knew he would go on to
become the England manager, or head coach as he was called
when he was in charge of the national side. Even then, way back
in the sixties, Terry had an aura about him. When he joined QPR
from Tottenham in 1969, everybody at Loftus Road went out of
their way to please him, from the manager Gordon Jago to Alec
Farmer the groundsman – and me, of course. Terry has a way of
making you want to earn his praise. It's a sign of his dominant
personality. With an ego to match.

Since I've known him, Terry has always been involved in
business ventures of some kind or another and contrary to what
some people may think, many have been successful. In those days
one of our regular drinking holes was the Rhinegold Club in
London's West End. On any given Saturday night, a gaggle of the
capital's footballers would be there. Geoff Hurst, Bobby Moore,
Mike England, Phil Beal, Alan Gilzean and Harry Redknapp
were among the regulars. Chelsea's Tommy Baldwin and Charlie

Cooke would often put in an appearance and countless others too numerous to mention. We'd drink way into the early hours, talk football, and laugh and joke. It was on one such night that I realised just how sharp Terry could be. In those days, he used to wear all the latest Italian suits, shoes and handmade shirts. He was a very handsome man, a really good-looking guy – not that he isn't now, of course. Terry was well aware of all this and it gave him a certain conceit and swagger.

After an away game one Saturday, we arrived back at Euston, jumped in taxis and were in the club by 10 p.m. I remember it vividly. We were sitting at the bar having a few drinks and Terry was immaculately dressed as usual with a brilliant white shirt and maroon tie. Not far away, a few young ladies were out on a hen night. I wasn't aware of them at first because I had my back to their table in the corner. Terry, though, had a splendid view of the girls, over my shoulder.

I was chatting away about the afternoon's match, the goals and the incidents and such. Terry wasn't saying a lot but every time I made a point he would give a disproportionate roar of laughter and one of his dazzling smiles. His big pearly whites were flashing so much I almost had to put sunglasses on. I remember thinking, 'Christ, Tel, it wasn't that funny.'

This went on for about 10 minutes until I suddenly realised that he wasn't looking at me but through me. When I looked around I could see Terry had been putting on a performance for the girls. I had to laugh. When I turned back I pointed my finger at him, Brian Clough style.

'You slippery bastard,' I laughed.

When we told all the other lads, they cracked up, especially Tony Hazell, the Rangers full-back, because the comment fitted him so perfectly. However, if the team caught up for a reunion, I think we would all agree that Terry should be the guest of honour.

Venables was born in Dagenham in 1943, a year before me.

He joined Chelsea when he was 15 where he became the youngest ever captain of a First Division side. In April of 1966 he went to Tottenham for £80,000, which opened the way for Charlie Cooke's move to Stamford Bridge from Dundee.

Before Terry was transferred to QPR three years later, he had become, and remains, the only player to be capped at every England representative level – schoolboy, youth, amateur and full international. He made his debut for England in 1964 against Belgium at Wembley after Bobby Charlton was injured. The fact that he got just one more cap doesn't do his talents justice. Terry was picked for a third international game but an injury let in Johnny Byrne who played well and stayed.

Venables, by his own admission, didn't do too well at White Hart Lane although he was selected for the initial 40 players of Alf Ramsey's 1966 World Cup squad. When Terry was at Rangers, it was said that Alf considered bringing him back because he had been playing better than at any of his previous clubs.

Venables later moved on to Crystal Palace where he ended his playing career. That's a story in itself. One day not long after Malcolm Allison had taken over at Selhurst Park, he called Terry into his office and told him quite bluntly that his days as a player were over. He was no longer up to it. Venables was around 30 at the time and was absolutely gutted by the news. Without a word of protest and in his own inimitable style, he got to his feet and walked slowly to the door. When he got there, he turned and said, 'Er, Malcolm . . . merry Christmas.' It was 24 December. When Terry told me that story I thought, 'Hey Malcolm, great timing pal!'

It was Allison, though, who gave Terry his start in management at Palace and never has there been a shrewder decision in football. Venables might well have been an excellent player but he was a much better coach. Years ago, Terry told me two things that are, apart from the obvious, the basis of successful management: you discover the strength of a team not when it is winning but when it is losing; and never make a rule you don't intend to keep. For instance, never set a curfew for 10.30 then tell the players it's OK to come back at midnight.

With these thoughts in mind, Venables took over from Allison in 1976 and led Palace from the Third to the First Division. Then in November 1980, Terry became QPR's manager when Tommy Docherty's abysmal second stint at Loftus Road came to an end. Four years later, Terry joined Barcelona where he was fabulously successful. However, in 1986, he missed out on a European Cup victory after the Spanish giants were beaten in a shoot-out by Steaua in Seville.

The following year Terry went to Tottenham and in 1991 became the club's chief executive. During that season, Spurs won the FA Cup with a 2–1 victory over Nottingham Forest after being one down at half-time. It was the White Hart Lane club's eighth success in the competition but Terry's celebrations were muted by Paul Gascoigne's horrendous challenge on Gary Charles, which put the future of the England star and Spurs' finances on hold for a while.

Terry is easily one of the brightest coaches the game has ever produced, which is why he was the popular and professionals' choice in 1994 to succeed Graham Taylor. Venables and the whole country endured another heartbreaking shoot-out in the 1996 European Championships when Germany, the eventual winners, beat us 6–5. England's tournament highlight was probably the 4–1 Gazza-inspired battering of Holland. That game illustrates just how far backwards we went afterwards. I'll never understand why the FA allowed Terry to leave after Euro 96. When you think about it, it's almost treasonable. After producing a side that did us all proud, those clowns at Lancaster Gate couldn't find a way to keep him. If they had, we wouldn't have gone through the farces that surrounded Glenn Hoddle and Kevin Keegan.

In spite of that decision, I believe Terry Venables still wants the opportunity to be remembered as the greatest England manager and a great football coach. However, the well-publicised financial and courtroom battles that led to his demise at Tottenham, ultimately undermined his position with the Football Association. He was unable to dissociate himself from that 'slippery spiv' image.

I find that very sad because I think people should be judged on how they do their job. Terry is a football man through and through and he wants to be successful in everything he does. But the media absolutely slaughtered him because of his dealings outside football and because he stuck with Eric Hall and Eddie Ashby. The press thought they were bad influences on him but Terry supported them for as long as he could out of genuine loyalty, and ended up being tarnished.

The FA blew a second chance to get Terry when they appointed Sven-Goran Eriksson. At the time of the appointment, in my honest opinion, Venables was the best man for the job. All the FA had to do was have Terry look after just the football side of England. That's all. After all, they didn't need him to take charge of the pension fund. Other tasks can be handled by the countless drones who inhabit Lancaster Gate. Consequently, he lost the opportunity to climb to the same heights as Sir Alf Ramsey. Incidentally, when Terry was young, he lived just a few streets away from Alf.

I clearly remember the day I realised Terry would be a top-class coach. It was when we were playing for QPR in an away game at Blackpool in 1969–70. We were losing and the manager, Gordon Jago, was giving his half-time talk. Gordon was a waffler. He was an FA coach and prone to using flowery language and missing the point. On this occasion he was jibbering on about it being a windy day, the pitch was bumpy so we couldn't pass it like we normally did and all sorts of meaningless stuff. When he finished he turned to Terry, who was the captain, and asked him if he had anything to say. Terry got up.

'OK,' he said. 'Their right full-back is getting too far forward and when he does Roger [Morgan] has got to go with him. On that free kick against us we had four men in the wall. When they have a dead-ball opportunity so close to our box like that we should have five. Parkesy [Phil Parkes, QPR's brilliant young goalkeeper], that's your responsibility. And when we go forward, the midfield has to support Rodney quicker because he's being left up there on his own.'

I thought, 'Christ Almighty!' Even then he was so clued up and in tune with everything. We all thought Terry was spot on. Even Jago sat back and listened with his mouth open. He couldn't put things as simply as that, but Terry could. When I went out for the second half, I recall thinking how good Terry was and I was so sure even then that he was going all the way.

One day at QPR after training we were practising volleys with Parkes in goal. We used to have a competition in which we would have 10 shots and then each player would give the attempt a mark out of 10. I always considered myself to be as skilful as any British player and my technique of volleying was second to none. Terry's was superb too, but he also liked to use a bit of gamesmanship, which he did on this occasion. Although Terry genuinely beat me, as he hit his 10th shot he shouted, 'Venables wins it again, eh?' That's an example of the sort of conceit and arrogance of somebody who has total self-belief. You can't knock it at all. I've always said that Terry's biggest asset is that he is not frightened of making mistakes.

When he first started playing football, he went into a business called Thingamywig, selling a hat and wig that women could wear after they had washed their hair and were waiting for it to dry. Terry and his partner sold three in a mail-order catalogue, but it never stopped him trying.

Terry has an array of talents in other areas apart from football. He has a fantastic singing voice, for instance, and I reckon he could have made it if he had chosen a recording career. He also wrote a novel with Gordon Williams called *They Used To Play On Grass*, and he helped pen 'Hazell', a TV detective series.

He got the name from Tony Hazell with whom he had many a ruck at Loftus Road.

Terry and I were introduced by a big Spurs punter called Maurice Keston and we would go to events at the Anglo-American sporting club, and at Phil Isaac's London Sportsman's club in Oxford Street. But we didn't become friends until Terry joined QPR when we hit it off straightaway. Jean and I frequently went to Terry and Chris's home in Loughton for dinner and they would come over to see us.

Every morning the Rat Pack would meet at the same café for breakfast and the only thing we'd talk about was football. What was going wrong or what was right. I sometimes wonder if players today are like that.

We would all socialise in those days. Jean and I became friends not only with Terry and Chris, but also with Bobby and Tina Moore, Geoff and Judith Hurst, Martin and Kathy Peters, George and Marie Graham, and Allan and Shirley Harris. The *Daily Mail* journalist Jeff Powell would also come along. Except for George, we were all from the East End and we got very close. Jean, Chris, Judith, Kathy and Tina would often go out together. But divorce can change a lot of things, which I find sad.

I never thought it would happen to Terry and Chris but it did. Terry always seemed so balanced and level-headed. I was the nutcase. I never dreamed he would fall in love with Toots and marry her. It changed the relationship that we had as a group. A second wife does not necessarily get on with the wives of her husband's friends because they knew the first one. That's what happened when Terry and Chris split up.

While Terry is very genuine and extremely loyal, if he thinks you have crossed him that's it. An example is Allan Harris. I feel, and it is only my opinion, the reason that Allan is no longer part of Terry's inner circle is because of some of the comments Shirley made about Terry and Toots. I think if she had just kept quiet,

Allan would have had a job for life as Terry's number two. But that's the way it goes.

Terry remarrying didn't affect our relationship. Wherever I was, we'd still meet up for a drink and a chat, often with Bobby Moore. We had one terrific Rat Pack lunch in a Kensington restaurant with Malcolm Allison, Terry, Mooro and me not long before Bobby died.

It's no secret that Terry has always been into money – like Bobby Keetch, the greatest 'spender' I ever met – and doing deals. On this occasion, I wanted to impress him by showing that I could wheel and deal successfully, too. During the meal we drank bottles of red wine and talked about football and where we'd all been in our careers. When the conversation turned to me in America, I said that I owned five houses. Sober, that sounds so boastful and brash yet all I was trying to do was mirror Terry; to curry favour by showing how much I had. After I'd finished speaking Mooro brought me straight down to earth.

'That must be a problem, Rod,' he said. 'How do you carry all those keys?'

Terry and I often had different opinions. When he first took over the England team I remember one discussion we had about his next game. I suppose he must have been getting it from all angles, like everyone else who has taken on the England manager's job. At the time, I felt he had made a couple of mistakes. The first was playing Alan Shearer up front on his own. I argued that, to produce his best, Shearer needed someone alongside him. Secondly, Terry had made David Platt his captain but I reckoned he would eventually have to give the job to Tony Adams.

'No I won't,' Terry argued. 'David Platt is a consummate professional.'

He is, of course. My point of view was that because David was involved in so much forward movement and wasn't in the hub of the action, it made the captaincy difficult for him; plus at the time David had injury problems.

I was proved right with Platt and Adams; Tony did take over the captaincy. But I was hopelessly wrong over Shearer. Terry, fortunately, stuck with his system of Shearer up front with Teddy Sheringham and Gascoigne behind him. Although Alan had a dry spell at first, it all came good during the Euro Championships. Terry had been spot on with that one.

Terry can be good at putting people in their place. He did it to me one night and I deserved it. We were having a drink in a London club, Morton's, with Jeff Powell. I was on a rant and said I thought it would be great if we could test our theories on football by being put in charge of teams that faced each other regularly. It's something we've never done.

'There's only one problem with that, Rod,' Terry said. 'You're not a manager.'

He was right. It's all very well having opinions but unless you put them into practice, that's all they are.

When people ask me if I have ever wanted to manage in the UK, my reaction is simple – are you mad? It doesn't appeal to me at all. I don't need the hassle. I had 11 great years coaching in Tampa but the game has changed so much here. A manager is under threat from fan power, player power, chairmen, plcs and not least, the mass media. A club can't be run in the way the manager wants any more. I watched Terry, Gerry Francis and Kevin Keegan visibly age under the strain and heard them ridiculed and abused. I've been asked to get involved by clubs in this country on a few occasions, but I'm happy with my TV work. I think I have a great job, why change it?

Behind all the confidence and self-belief, Terry has another, more emotional, side. He was good to me when my father died.

After the umbrella incident early on in my career when my mum smacked an opposing fan in the face in rage, I refused to let my parents watch me again. I know my dad came on different occasions throughout my whole career but I never knew when he was coming and he never asked me for tickets. He told me later that sometimes he went in disguise, like he did when I was a kid, which when you think about it is comical. He used to coach me every day when I was a kid and have me running up and down the street training. He was desperate for me to be a footballer. I guess it was hardly surprising that he wanted to watch me play once I had made it.

When I lived in London I saw my mum and dad every week but on moving to Manchester it became less frequent, though Jean and I still tried to make sure that the children saw them every month. Either we went down to London or they came up to us. When I moved to the States we saw them when we came home. I offered to move them over to Tampa but they said no. They didn't want to leave their home over here.

My mum died when she was 56 from a brain tumour. She had been ill for a little while and suffering from dizzy spells. She saw a doctor but was initially misdiagnosed as suffering from vertigo. As her condition deteriorated and she began to suffer severe headaches, she went for a second opinion, which found that she had a massive brain tumour behind her eyes that was inoperable. Not only that, they discovered she had lung cancer which had spread to all parts of her body. Both my mother and father were very heavy smokers. I was in America at the time and I kept flying home, every time thinking it would be the last time I saw her. She died in hospital about six months after she was diagnosed. I had flown in a week before and sat with her during her final days.

My father was devastated by her death and so I took over all the funeral arrangements and sorted out everything that needed to be done. He never really recovered from losing her. It was just over a year later, in 1981, that he died from a stroke.

I was in the country at the time. I had come over to visit him, but Jean and the kids were still in the States. I went to see him on the Friday morning and it was on that occasion that he went to hug me and I couldn't hug him back. We spent all day together just talking about what had been happening, how the kids were and what I was up to in America. On the Saturday I had arranged to go to watch QPR. I often went on my own but, looking back now, I regret so much not asking my dad to go with me that day. As I arrived at the ground a policeman came up to me and said, 'Could I have a quiet word with you?' I said of course, thinking I had parked my car in the wrong place or something like that; but as he carried on I knew it was more than that.

'Would you like to sit down?' he asked.

'Why?' I asked. 'What's happened?'

'Your father's dead.'

Just like that, that's how he said it. I know there is no easy way to say it but it was so hard and cold. For the next few days I was in a trance. I desperately regretted not making peace with my father and then suddenly he was dead.

I had fallen out with almost all of my relatives over the way they treated Dad after my mother passed away. With me away in America, I thought they could have looked after him a bit, but they hadn't bothered. Some of them telephoned and asked me where and when the funeral was. I told them to fuck off, nobody was invited and I would handle all my dad's arrangements on my own the following week. As far as I was, and still am, concerned it will be too soon if I ever speak to them again.

Several days later, Terry rang and I gave him my usual greeting. I hadn't spoken to Terry for a while and I was touched when he said, 'I hope you don't mind, Rod. I hope you're not offended but I'd like to come to your father's funeral.'

I told Terry that he would be welcome and gave him the details. At the church there was just Dad, me, a couple of my close friends, the vicar and Terry, who sat at the back by himself without saying a word. He had just come to pay his respects. It was so nice of him to be there. In my eyes, Terry was immediately elevated. He had no reason to come but he wanted to be there for me. It was a brilliant gesture. Afterwards, Dad's ashes were scattered on the rose garden outside the church and I was devastated because I had lost both my parents within 18 months. So Terry took me out that night and we got drunk together. We never spoke about that day again and his actions showed what a good person he is.

About a year later I was back coaching in America. Before an away game in Buffalo, New York, I was woken in my hotel room by the telephone. It was probably around two or three in the morning. It was Terry.

'Rod,' he said. 'It's Terry.' He was in tears.

'What's happened, Tel?' I asked. He told me that Dave Clement, the former QPR and England full-back, had committed suicide.

'I didn't want you to find out any other way,' he said. 'I wanted to let you know personally because I didn't want you to hear it from someone else.' Then he put the phone down.

I sat up in bed for hours thinking how remarkable that was. For Terry to find me in the first place was amazing. I could have been anywhere in the world and he must have made several calls to discover what I was doing. I don't think I'd spoken to him since my dad's funeral. To go to those lengths, and the fact that he was so upset, show another side of Terry that people don't see. It's important to me that people should understand the sort of man he is. It's why players at all of the clubs he has been in charge of, and England players, think so highly of him. If he did those kind of things with me, he must have done them for other people too.

Things are different between Terry and me now, ever since we had one incredible row at his old Knightsbridge nightclub, Scribes, that almost turned into a fight. It was when Terry was having major problems with Sir Alan Sugar, just before he was sacked by Tottenham in May 1993. I personally thought the whole affair at Spurs was being blown out of all proportion.

When the feud was at its peak, I said on a Sky television programme that I thought, even though Terry was in the right, for the good of everybody he should apologise to Alan Sugar and move forward because all the publicity was hurting everybody. Neither of them would back down and the fact that the case was going to court was hampering Terry's career. When I made that statement, I half hoped it would get the media on Terry's side. Then, perhaps, Alan Sugar might be the one to back down. I was trying to play some reverse psychology but it backfired on me.

Terry had been watching the programme and he was fuming about my comments. Later, about 10.30 that night, I got a phone call from Mary Shatali who told me she had had a drink with Terry earlier in the evening. He hadn't calmed down one bit and was still foaming at the mouth, she said. When I hung up the phone I decided to deal with the situation in the only way I knew how. I believe that if there's a problem, you have to get it sorted as soon as you can. My attitude is always tell it like it is and when in doubt, tell the truth. So I picked up the phone, rang Scribes and got straight through to Terry.

'I understand you've got a problem with me,' I said.

'I have got a fucking problem with you,' Terry replied.

I asked him how long he was going to be there and when he told me all night I said I'd be there in half an hour. So right away I jumped in my car and drove to Scribes. When I walked in, Terry looked at me and in front of everybody said, 'What the fuck are you doing?'

'Hey, Tel, not here,' I answered. He grabbed hold of my arm and marched me into one of the offices and closed the door.

We were in there for half an hour screaming at each other. His point was that he couldn't in the world understand why, as a close friend, I would think he was the one who should stand down. Alan Sugar had done this and done that.

'I would rather stick red hot pins in my own eyes than

apologise to him,' Terry shouted. 'Can't you see that, you stupid bastard.' On and on he went.

Again, I explained my view. I had always been and always will be supportive of Terry but he just wouldn't have it. So in a very manly and gentlemanly manner we shook hands and agreed to disagree. For a long time afterwards we didn't really speak, and when we did it was frosty between us. That didn't stop me from supporting him professionally on 'Soccer Saturday'. And I'm happy to say that I recently caught up with him again, after he had helped Middlesbrough to stay in the Premiership, and it seemed that we were finally able to get things back to how they used to be. I'm sure we haven't seen the last of Terry as a top-level coach.

the greatest footballer who ever lived

*There's only one thing I want on my headstone and that's
'Here lies George Best, the greatest footballer who ever lived.'*

George Best, 1994

I know how it began – and I know how it will end, too. I'll say a few words at his funeral, or maybe he will at mine. In my case, it will be by invitation or just because I want to. People need to know how the real George Best wants to be remembered. You see, what worries me is that a lot of people won't know or understand the real Besty.

I was in America when I first got the news about George's collapse with liver failure. I immediately called his agent Phil Hughes.

'It's not good, Marshy,' he said. 'Keep your fingers crossed, pal.'

It was as bad as that. Phil has always been extremely positive about George so I knew by the sound of his voice that this time it was a desperate situation. We had a short chat and he told me what details he could. After five minutes or so he had to hang up as he was due to visit George in the emergency room at London's Cromwell Hospital.

As soon as I got back to the UK, I called Phil again to make sure it was OK to go to the hospital.

'George said he'd like to see you when you can,' he said, which was a lot better news than I had anticipated. The mind can play a lot of tricks, especially when someone is as sick as George was then. For all that, I went to the Cromwell Hospital the next day not knowing what I would find. When I got there, I pushed my way through the crowd of photographers, and they shouted at me, 'Rod, tell us how he is? When is he coming out?'

'For Christ's sake,' I thought. 'Let's just hope he makes it.' Walking up to the hospital doors and past the security guards, whom I assumed were posted to keep out those parasites, I had too much on my mind to say anything. At the reception area, I introduced myself – 'Rodney Marsh to see George Best.' After a telephone call to George's room, I was allowed to proceed. Phil and Alex, Besty's wife, hadn't arrived and when I nervously knocked on the door of George's room, I had a horrible feeling in my gut.

'Come in,' called George and I pushed open the door. I braced myself but I wasn't anywhere near prepared for what I saw. I tried not to react yet I couldn't help a lump forming in my throat as I set eyes on my old pal. The last time I had seen him, about three weeks earlier at Sky Sports, we both had a large glass of white wine in our hands and were laughing and joking about the cock-up we had made on 'Soccer Saturday' that afternoon. I couldn't believe how much George had changed in such a short space of time. He had lost two and a half stone, had several tubes in his arm and his face was a putrid dark yellow. The sight of George almost brought tears to my eyes. He looked so frail, so wasted. Still, he was chirpy. He gave me one of his smashing smiles and told me in great detail what had happened and what the prognosis was for the future.

'Let's get a cup of tea in the canteen,' he said. 'It's shit but at least it will get me moving.'

I helped George on with his dressing gown and opened the door, not knowing if he was allowed to leave the room or not.

After shuffling the 60 feet or so to the tea-room, Besty slumped exhausted into one of the canteen chairs. I honestly thought he was going to die there in hospital.

Alex and Phil showed up soon after that and we all had a cup of tea and made half-hearted funny comments. I stayed about an hour, chatting and doing my best to put on a brave face for George before pushing my way once more through the crowds and going back to my flat. On the way home tears filled my eyes because I really thought I'd seen George for the last time. But I hadn't, thank God.

A few days later I called Phil for an update.

'Pop in when you like, Rod. George is feeling a bit better,' he said. 'Call first though.'

I did and went back twice more before he was discharged 10 days later. Once again it appeared that Besty had beaten the odds and proved everybody wrong.

Later in the year, I had a most illuminating conversation with George. By then he had been to Spain for a break after a much-publicised night of madness back on the booze. Thankfully, the lapse didn't last and he had recovered enough to appear again on our 'Soccer Saturday' show. He was still incredibly under-weight and fragile but as bright as ever. After the show, we sat in the production office at Sky, just him and me. He was very focused yet melancholy.

'You wanna see the place I've bought in Northern Ireland, Marshy,' he told me. 'Miles from anywhere. Beautiful little cottage, right on the sea. Me and Alex are gonna renovate it, get some antiques, snooker table, dart board and everything. Come over for a weekend whenever you want.'

'What are you doing about the flat in Chelsea?' I asked.

'Selling it,' he said. 'Gonna move full time to Ireland.'

It struck me that George was going home to die.

Over the years when we've been alone in the back of taxis and limos, sometimes both stone cold sober I might add, we used to talk about our families, our hopes and dreams, where we were going in life and what's important. He would talk about his love for Callum, his son. He would always ask about my children, totally different from the image and perception that people have of him.

We didn't actually meet until the summer following my 1972 move to Manchester City and after George's first retirement from United. We had both played in a charity match in the city. George had turned out for a side from his nightclub, Slack Alice, and I had lined up for C'est La Vie, a wine bar owned by Max Brown, a big City punter and entrepreneur. In those days, the whole of Manchester was either red or blue and Max was 100 per cent blue.

Geoff Baker, a former rugby player and a major local night-lifer who took care of rock bands when they were in the north, introduced us. I'm delighted to say that Geoff remains a close friend of Besty's and mine to this day.

Anyway, we said hello and smiled. Then I got one of the biggest shocks I've ever had in my life. When we shook hands, I'll never forget the look in his eyes. They were as clear as crystal and instantly said, 'Don't fuck with me.' I was invading his territory. I think George might have seen me as a bit of a threat because City were much more successful than United in those days. At the time, I wasn't sure I had read his look correctly but I later found out I had been spot-on. That message was precisely what he meant. After that first meeting, I thought we had more chance of becoming arch-enemies than mates.

We bumped into each other from time to time when we were out and about in Manchester. Unfortunately, on one of those nights I had been on a lunatic drinking binge. It started after I scored one of City's goals in a victory over United at Old Trafford; it ended with me trashing George's Slack Alice bar.

The derby victory had the City fans celebrating in the streets and a crowd of us arrived at George's club around 3 a.m. I was right out of order. For a start, I didn't like the music the disc jockeys were playing, so I took over their booth and played all my favourites. Then, while the music I had chosen was blaring out, I smashed all the records that I hated on the dance floor. What a complete and outright arsehole I was that night!

Colin Byrne, George's partner, sat watching in amazement. After my cameo performance I started dancing with Geoff, a big Manchester United fan. He was as drunk as I was and couldn't bear to watch me gloating over City's performance so he slapped me in the face. Within seconds we were butting each other and rolling over tables and chairs. It was like a scene out of the movies. It only ended when I crashed a potted tree over Geoff's head and the dirt and fragments went everywhere. I thought I'd killed him, but he just burst out laughing. I later found out that the manager had called the police but when the special constable arrived and asked about the trouble, George and Colin just said, 'Trouble? What trouble?' gave him a quick drink and sent him on his way.

That was the beginning of our friendship. I respected George for the way he handled the situation that night and the respect has lasted ever since.

I learned more about George at Fulham. One night, after an evening match at Craven Cottage, Bobby Moore, George and I went out for a drink. George and I were on white wine and Mooro was on lager. Eventually, we ended up in Tramp, George's favourite London club. We were regulars and there were frequent drinking contests, although you had to be mad to get into one of those with George and Bobby.

In the seventies, Tramp was the place to be because that's where you'd find all the top footballers along with rock and movie stars. Johnny Gold, the owner, was a closet Spurs fan if ever there was one. Still, nobody's perfect and we all enjoyed his fabulous hospitality.

That evening Besty was like a man on a mission and after

about an hour, during a lull in conversation, I made the mistake of offering him some advice.

'George,' I suggested, 'why don't you get something to eat. You haven't eaten all day.' It was the worst piece of counselling anyone has given. George turned to me and his eyes flashed in just the same way as they had when we met.

'Don't you fucking ever tell me what to do!' he shouted.

Mooro's mouth dropped open and you could have heard a pin drop. I realised I had overstepped the bounds of our friendship. Nevertheless, I still found it in me to snap back, 'All right, please your fucking self.' We have never spoken about this incident. Friends are the people you can be yourself with and who take you for what you are. I learned that George only did what he wanted to do and nobody would ever change that.

George is a very intelligent man, has an opinion about most things, is well read, articulate and, unless provoked, extremely well mannered; and he is completely in control of what he does. Besty has always been in charge of his own destiny. He is nowhere near the tragic figure he is painted. George knows, and has known for most of his life, the result of excessive drinking. It's still the path he chose.

The thing that has always staggered me is the incredible amount of attention he gets wherever he goes. A few years ago we were on the way to Belfast from London's Heathrow Airport and George could hardly get on the plane because of the constant hounding for his autograph. Not once did he refuse. The point is, that's what it's like for him wherever he goes. He can't go out and not be accosted by people who want to buy him a drink. In my opinion, for what it's worth, George elected to drink to anaesthetise himself from the overwhelming media and public attention.

The attraction is not all idolatry either. One night he was in a club having a quiet drink and without warning someone smashed a pint glass over his head. The blow knocked George unconscious and he was rushed to hospital where 25 stitches were inserted in the wound. He had no idea why it happened. It was just an idiot trying to make a name for himself. It shows you the sort of thing that can happen to George that is not of his own making. Everywhere Besty has gone he's had to face situations like that and it creates the kind of pressure that would get anybody down.

Think about it. One minute people are buying you drinks and all over you; then when you least expect it, someone tries to kill you. Remember the time when George was punched in the face while he was sitting in his car at traffic lights? Some bloke decided to chin him because he had a Jaguar. Unbelievable!

That sort of attention would turn a saint to drink. To a degree I can understand what it's like and that is why I can appreciate what drove George to the bottle.

David Beckham is, I suppose, considered to be the closest thing to George from the modern game. He has the looks, the famous wife, the talent and he plays for Manchester United. But he seems a very level-headed lad with a supportive family around him. He hasn't moved away from his roots and has been protected a great deal by his manager Sir Alex Ferguson. Both he and George suffer from constant media attention but George is and was very different from David Beckham.

If anything, the only player comparable to George in recent years is Gazza. When he burst on to the scene after Italia 90 as a 21-year-old, the media attention was staggering. Instantly, he became a worldwide name. He didn't have the same kind of pin-up image as George, but he was in the paper every day as much for his off-the-field antics as for his football. They were both on-field geniuses with flawed personalities and alcohol has played a major part in their lives. Maradona has gone the same way, but his downfall has been with drugs. David Beckham is a great footballer but doesn't have that genius mentality that Best, Maradona and Gazza had. He hasn't reached the heights of adulation that George experienced when he was at United.

Over the years, George and I have had some great fun together and we've always laughed a lot. George is great company, he loves a joke and has a fantastic sense of humour. In the right surroundings, he is the centre of the conversation and far removed from the way he has been portrayed as a gambler, a drunk and a womaniser. When a cartoon appeared caricaturing him as a drunk peering up through a manhole with a bottle of champagne in his hand, George and his father, Dickie, were really upset about it.

During the roadshow years, obviously we saw a lot of each other. Once, we ended up playing pool in Rag's, the sister nightclub to Tramp off London's Curzon Street, where we had gone for a nightcap and a bite to eat after a gig. About three in the morning we left to go home and as we walked down the road to get a taxi, George spotted a homeless guy in a shop doorway. It was a bitterly cold night so he stopped, pulled a £50 note from his pocket and with a smile gave it to the man. At first I thought George had mistakenly given the man more than he intended but he hadn't. He knew well enough the amount he had handed over. It was typical of George. Deep down he is a very humble person. We've never spoken about that night either, but my respect for him grew.

Many celebrities love being around soccer players. Most are fine. Phil Collins is a big QPR fan. He invited me to the premiere of the film *Buster* in which he starred and that was great. We even had a chat at the reception afterwards. Then there's Rod Stewart, a mad Celtic and Manchester United follower who adores Denis Law; and, of course, Elton John's enthusiasm for the game is well known.

But they're not all like that. George once told me about the night he went to Tramp with his former wife Angie and Bobby Moore. The champagne had, as usual, been flowing and they were having a great time with Johnny Gold until a very famous actor came to the table with his wife. At first it was very convivial and they were asking Besty and Mooro questions about football and generally talking about the game. But then he said something that annoyed George because he felt it insulted Angie. Admittedly, it had been in drink but George still said to him, 'You'd better take that back. You don't say things like that to ladies.'

The actor didn't apologise. So George told him he had to, or he would do something about it – and he meant it. When he once more declined and stole some French fries from George's plate in a gesture of defiance, Besty slapped him on the side of the head with the back of his hand. The blow knocked him backwards, so the waiters had to come round and calm things down.

You hear so many stories about George taking advantage of women but he is always a gentleman in their company, and he insists that others are too.

I find it very interesting that people today rarely mention just how dedicated George was to football. There was nobody who trained harder or longer, and nobody cared more for the team or about winning. George always tried to do the right things. Unfortunately, everything he did off the pitch seemed to go a bit wonky.

People still insist that he is a tragic figure but I say this – nobody has given more pleasure to football fans than he has and that's all that matters. People who say differently don't know what they are talking about. Only now have I come to recognise the real sense of the history and legend that is George Best.

So how would George like to be remembered? It's not how the media circus would like to remember him.

One night we appeared before a packed crowd of QPR supporters at the Beck Theatre in Hayes. In the limo on our way home George said to me, 'You know, Marshy, when it's all over and everyone has written about the birds, the booze and the gambling, there's only one thing I want on my headstone and that's "Here lies George Best, the greatest footballer who ever lived".'

If I write his epitaph he'll get his wish, but I hope it's a very, very long way off.

CHAPTER 13

now that's a team

You hope and you pretend you know what you are doing.

Kevin Keegan, on the art of football management

Terry Venables once wrote a book called *The Best Game in the World*. The best game, apart from football itself of course, for players and fans alike is picking your favourite team. It happens in pubs and clubs around the country. Over the last four decades I've discussed great players with many equally great players, the likes of Terry, Besty and Mooro. We've spent countless hours selecting our All-Time side.

For fun, I've picked a side from all those people I've played with and against, which doesn't make it any easier because during my time in America the NASL was, as I've said before, a Who's Who of magnificent players.

The manager, without a shadow of a doubt, would be Sir Alf Ramsey because his record with England stands up against anybody's. There's been nobody like Sir Alf and there probably never will be. With Ramsey, failure wasn't an option. I have never met anybody more single-minded. It was always his way – or the highway. The only ricket I think he made was when he took off Bobby Charlton in the 1970 World Cup quarter-final, which I have mentioned a couple of times before. But Bobby was 32 at the time and Alf's decision is easy to understand.

When Ramsey was in charge you were never in doubt about what he wanted. Everybody knew their job and took it very seriously indeed. Footballers will always be footballers, though, and when I won my caps we all used to take the mickey out of Alf for being so straight and proper – but not to his face because he didn't have a sense of humour, or at least, not one I could see.

In goal would be Gordon Banks. Gordon, who won 73 caps for England, is not the greatest ever goalkeeper like a lot of people think. In my view, that accolade goes to Peter Schmeichel. There's a strong possibility that Sir Alex Ferguson might not have got a knighthood if the Great Dane had chosen to stay at Brondby in 1991. That's how highly I rate Schmeichel. But I didn't play in Peter's era, and he is only just a little ahead of Banks. What is remarkable about the former Chesterfield, Leicester and Stoke No. 1 is that he played at a time when there were a lot of other superb goalkeepers around, including Ray Clemence, Peter Shilton, Pat Jennings, Alex Stepney and Peter Bonetti. What makes me an authority on all these guys? That's easy. I scored against all of them. They were all fantastic in their own way. Jennings, for instance, was unbelievable at handling crosses.

What puts Banks just ahead of his contemporaries is that he made everything look so simple. Gordon's shot-stopping abilities were the best I have ever seen – apart from Schmeichel – and his distribution was superb. So much so that he hardly ever wasted possession. Banks was tremendously brave and he had great balance when it wasn't as important as it is today. He also had the sort of intuitive reactions that can make the difference between winning and losing.

For 10 years Banks wasn't just the best goalkeeper in Britain, he was the best in the world – a far cry from his early days when he was kicked out of his Yorkshire League youth team for letting in 15 goals in two games. Gordon later admitted, 'I was noted more for the alacrity with which I picked balls out of the back of my net than for any stopping ability.'

Banks became a coalman and an apprentice bricklayer before laying the foundation on which England won the 1966 World Cup. Who can possibly forget the way he denied Pele in the 1970 World Cup in Mexico? Everyone refers to that moment now as 'the save'. A few years ago I wrote a foreword for a book entitled *One Hundred Great Football Moments in World Cup History* and Banks's scoop off the line was the first on my list. Pele has watched it hundreds of times and he still can't believe how Gordon pulled it off.

Tragically, Gordon lost the sight in one of his eyes in a car accident in 1972. That may have ended his career in England but Banks went to America where, with just the one eye, he was still a better keeper than anyone else around and that's a fact. When Gordon was with the Fort Lauderdale Strikers he almost single-handedly got them to an NASL championship playoff semi-final and was voted the League's Most Valuable Goalkeeper in 1977. To carry on playing at a decent level with that sort of handicap is a tribute in itself. Gordon stopped me from scoring on hundreds of occasions. I beat him five or six times only.

When I first played for England in 1971 I roomed with Banks. I was the new kid on the block and I think Alf Ramsey wanted him to take me under his wing. Unfortunately, I never had a proper conversation with Gordon in the 48 hours we were together. I probably called him 'Mr Banks'. But Gordon was a brilliant team player, just the sort of person you'd want in the dressing-room because of his fantastic attitude. He has been a credit to football in every way and I don't think anyone would argue with that.

Then, lining up in a 4-3-3 formation, I would start at right-back with Carlos Alberto. I played against him many times in America when he was with the New York Cosmos and I was at the Rowdies. Carlos was such a talented man and so good he could have played in any position. For all that, the Brazilian captain was frequently criticised for his lack of defensive skills, which is a point I understand but don't accept.

Great players play to their limitations. I know that might sound strange but, for instance, people said Bobby Moore wasn't quick enough, didn't know how to head a ball and couldn't tackle. I remember hearing those things on so many occasions when I was at Fulham in the early sixties, but we all know the heights Bobby scaled. Sometimes it annoys me when people try to dig out the negative aspects of a player. What made Mooro so brilliant was his uncanny anticipation and you don't learn that from any coaching manual. As Jock Stein once said, 'There ought to be a law against Moore. He knows what's happening twenty minutes before anyone else!'

I can't believe it when, even today, people say that Carlos Alberto had weaknesses – he skippered Brazil's 1970 World Cup-winning side which was arguably the best international side ever! The build-up to his fourth goal in the final against Italy was brilliant. What's the point of worrying about defending when you can attack like him?

Alberto was rarely put under pressure at international level because he had so many great players around him. Brazilian teams nearly always play with a spare man at the back so when Alberto moved forward their system was able to cope; and it meant the attacker he was marking had to become a defender. For that style to work properly, you've got to have top-class players around you.

In the middle of defence would be Franz Beckenbauer and Bobby Moore. There's not much between these two fabulous centre-backs. Over the years I've often been asked whom I thought was better and it's a good question.

I twice played against Beckenbauer for England when the Kaiser was in his prime; and I played against him on countless occasions in the States when Franz was with the Cosmos. In those days, he used to mark me and I'm pleased to say I scored quite a few times against him. Actually, that goes for Bobby too.

When I first saw Beckenbauer in 1966 he was marking Bobby Charlton and that is the reason West Germany lost the World Cup final. Maybe the Germans were a little in awe of Bobby, and rightly so because he was a world-class player.

Beckenbauer was a genius. He had tremendous vision and his skill at interception was equalled only by Bobby Moore. The only player to get anywhere near either of them in recent years, although never that close, is Italy's Franco Baresi. The thing about great defenders like Franz and Bobby was that they knew exactly when to dive into the tackle and when to back off. Rio Ferdinand looks as if he has a chance of emulating the way Moore and Beckenbauer used the ball. The question is, can he learn to intercept like them?

Bobby played in an era of super tough defenders, Norman Hunter and Ron Harris to name but two, and what made him different was that he could not only smarten you up but front you up as well. Let me explain. A lot of players around then would tackle from behind or the side and go right through you. But Mooro and Tommy Smith could also go face to face with you for a fifty-fifty ball. A lot of defenders don't like to do that. They are much happier doing things you can't see. They might top you up but they'll always duck it when it gets naughty. Bobby Moore never did cowardly things on the pitch, or off it come to that.

You might think my pairing of Mooro and Beckenbauer lacks height. Of course, the ideal central defender would be a cross between Beckenbauer, Mooro and Jack Charlton but there wasn't one around in my day so I'm picking the next best option.

Bobby Moore was simply a giant among men. To me, he was the apotheosis of a true English gentleman. I really got to know him well when we started going to a little pub on Hampstead Heath on Sunday mornings and it was during those meetings that I began to realise how different he was.

Let me give you an example. In 1971 I went to Greece with England. Although I was in the 22-man squad, I wasn't one of the

16 players and therefore didn't participate in the game. I did everything else with the team, including training and socialising. After the game, which we won 2–0 thanks to goals from Geoff Hurst and Martin Chivers, a dozen of us, including Mike Summerbee, Franny Lee, Bobby and me, went to a taverna for a meal. We had a great time and when I hear people talking about the roaring seventies, this night always comes flooding back. We had a victory to celebrate and plenty of readies from a boot sponsorship deal that we were spending like there was no tomorrow. The Dom Perignon was flowing like one of the fountains around Athens' Constitution Square. We drank and drank then drank some more until everyone was upside down.

Well, we all know what you look like the morning after a night like that. When I woke and looked in the mirror my eyes were like slits. With my hands shaking, I cut myself shaving so many times I had to put little bits of paper all over my face to stop the bleeding. My mouth was like the bottom of a bird's cage. I looked a mess. We all did. But at breakfast, there was Bobby sitting in a neatly pressed black blazer and a sparkling white shirt that almost blinded me. His face looked as if it had been ironed. Mooro didn't look as if he'd been out at all.

Dehydrated, I headed straight for some iced water that was on the table. As I grasped the bottle, Bobby coolly looked up and gave his usual catchphrase greeting, 'Marshy? All is well?' I couldn't even open my mouth. Bobby may well still have been legless but he always looked a million dollars in any situation.

As I'm sure has become clear from reading this book, Bobby Moore is one of my all-time heroes, as a player and as a person. Even though others were closer to Bobby than I was, I got to know him particularly well in Charlotte. I had the utmost respect for him because he confronted his problems on and off the pitch with a dignity and a pride that a lot of people, not just footballers, would do well to study. I have never been in his class and never will be.

Franz and Bobby were arch-enemies on the pitch but they were great buddies off it and would regularly have dinner at each other's houses. I had a chat with Franz at Bobby's funeral in 1993. We had only shaken hands before and when we found ourselves standing next to each other, I asked Beckenbauer if he remembered me.

'I know who you are, Rodney,' he replied. 'I remember you from the Tampa Bay Rowdies and you were always a problem for us.'

The No. 3 shirt would go to another German icon, Paul Breitner. In 48 appearances for West Germany between 1971 and 1982, Breitner scored 10 goals, which is a better haul than some of England's current forwards. Breitner was a breathtaking full-back at a time when the German side was full of great players. His runs and shots were almost as good as Carlos Alberto's. In fact, he started his career in the No. 2 berth. In the current game, Denis Irwin is not dissimilar to him, a right-footed player playing left-back. Paul was in that mould – very reliable and dependable, not outstanding, but a player you would want in your team. A deadly spot-kick taker, it was his penalty that earned West Germany's equaliser against Holland in the 1974 World Cup final, and his surging runs set up their 2–1 victory.

Breitner was a bit of a maverick off the pitch. He nearly became the German team manager, but the offer was quickly withdrawn after he launched one of his trademark blistering attacks on the national federation.

On the right side of midfield I would have the incomparable Johnny Haynes. Johnny was simply magnificent in every sense of the word. I've seen a lot of players over the years and for me, Haynes was the best passer of the ball there has ever been, from any country. His distribution was unique. The only person in recent years to get anywhere close to Johnny was Glenn Hoddle. The main difference between them was that Haynes scored more goals and he played in two World Cup finals. Johnny had amazing vision, and he was one of football's gentlemen in days when sportsmanship and fair play meant a whole lot more than they do today. His only weakness was that he wasn't the bravest header of the ball – perhaps, as the first Brylcreem Boy, he didn't want to mess up his hair!

Alongside Johnny in the central midfield berth would be Bobby Charlton who was the greatest midfield player that Britain has ever produced, without a shadow of a doubt. Not only that, Bobby was probably the best naturally two-footed player in the history of the game. Charlton could score goals with sheer power, with either foot, from up to 40 yards. When he was young, it was difficult to recognise which of his feet was better. He could also go past defenders on either side – and what about his blistering free kicks. He was a midfielder and is still English football's top scorer at international level, which shows what an amazing player he was.

Talented as David Beckham is, he could never do what Bobby did in the centre of the park. Charlton was so comfortable with both feet, he didn't have to stop and think. If a pass was on, he just played it. What would England give for someone like that today. Paul Scholes pops up with goals from midfield but they aren't similar players. Bobby Charlton combined the best of Beckham and Scholes.

I remember one of Bobby's tremendous two goals against Portugal that put England in the 1966 World Cup final. Running on to a ball that had been pulled back by Geoff Hurst, Charlton hammered it into the far corner. Even the Portuguese players, including the great Eusebio, applauded the effort, and some shook Bobby's hand as he trotted back to the centre circle. There's another example of how the game has changed.

Bobby could run with the ball and run off the ball; his movement was supreme and he could find spaces where none existed. If he was man-marked, lots of luck to his marker because he could always find a way to escape. Charlton had such a great engine that he ran Beckenbauer ragged on quite a few occasions. And contrary to what some people might say, I think he showed a lot of finesse when heading the ball. He put Manchester United into the lead with a headed goal in the 1968 European Cup final against Benfica.

But Bobby couldn't tackle, which I found out during my first Manchester derby. I played my first four or five games for City when not 100 per cent fit. A groin strain I had picked up at QPR made it difficult for me to train properly. So against United I started on the bench and watched them score before we equalised. The atmosphere at Old Trafford was incredible, electrifying. It's a buzz that's difficult to explain unless you've actually played in a game like that.

With 20 minutes to go, Malcolm Allison told me to warm up along the touchline and as I did so, the Manchester United fans chanted 'Rodney is a fairy, Rodney is a fairy'. On hearing this, the City fans at the other end retaliated with an 'Oh, Rodney, Rodney . . .' The barracking grew into a crescendo and the game almost became secondary.

When I eventually pulled off my tracksuit I felt super-charged. I had a little bit of a sweat on and in spite of a light drizzle I was fired up to go. Three minutes later, Summerbee went on a run down the right-hand side and when he pulled the ball back to the edge of the box, I was waiting. With my first touch of the match, I clipped the ball hard and low and it flew past Alex Stepney and straight into the United goal. In celebration, I ran over to the United supporters at the Stretford End, waggled my backside and sang 'Oh, Rodney, Rodney . . .' At this, the Old Trafford fans went mental and tried to climb over the fence to get at me. It was amazing.

With minutes to go and 2–1 up, I received a pass on the right wing and Bobby came over to cover me. I pushed the ball past him but as I went to go by the great man I accidentally kicked him on the ankle as he tackled me. After the clash I took a dive, and Bobby went ballistic when the ref gave a foul against him. He was moaning like Albert Tatlock until I told him, 'Shut up, Bob, for Christ's sake.' That wasn't the end of it. Colin Bell took the resulting free kick, Franny Lee got a flick and wallop, the ball was in the net, and Bobby was still vehemently protesting to the official. It was hilarious.

From the kick-off we immediately got the ball back and I went on a run towards the United goal. On the way, Bill Foulkes slid in but missed me. We were now in injury time and instead of going directly for goal, I ran with the ball towards the corner flag as a snorting Nobby Stiles chased me. Just before I got there, I stopped and dragged the ball back, which sent Nobby flying on to the running track around the pitch. At the flag, with the ball at my feet, I put one hand on the corner post and looked at an imaginary watch on my other wrist and screamed at the United fans, 'How long to go?' Afterwards I realised how close I had come to inciting a riot, but hey, they started it.

You can't have a greatest side without George Best. He would wear the No. 11 shirt and play on the left-hand side of midfield. For two years Besty was the greatest player in the world. During that period he was completely unstoppable. Kicking him didn't work, either – ask Ron Harris or Norman Hunter and they will tell you that if you did that to George he would kick back twice as hard. Besty was never a soft player.

When he first came on the scene as a 17-year-old in the 1963–64 season, nobody could believe how quick he was. There were some fast full-backs around then, such as George Cohen who was exceptional, and Besty gave them all a torrid time. He was a genius with two great feet and terrific heading ability. There hasn't been a player to compare with him since. Ryan Giggs is often likened to him, but he doesn't come close. George had everything. Unless you saw him you can't comprehend just how good he was. Most of his games weren't even captured on camera. When Manchester United fans voted Eric Cantona the best player in their history it was a joke. Cantona was nowhere near as good as George. Every 50 years or so a true genius comes along and that was George.

Sir Alex Ferguson paid him a fine tribute as a player when he said, 'George was unique, the greatest talent our football ever produced, easily. Look at his scoring record – 137 goals in 361 league games and a total of 179 goals for United in 466 matches. That's phenomenal for a man who did not get the share of gift goals that comes to specialist strikers. George nearly always had to beat men to score.'

The first of my front three would be Johan Cruyff, the total footballer, another natural leader who could do anything. He was also probably one of the most intelligent footballers ever. When I was at Manchester City, we played Barcelona in a pre-season friendly. Cruyff had joined them from Ajax for almost a million pounds – incidentally his share of the transfer was £400,000! Before the match at the Nou Camp there was a knock on our dressing-room door. When I opened it, Johan formally intro-duced himself and asked who was our captain.

'Very pleased to meet you,' I replied. 'That's me. I'm Rodney Marsh.'

'Welcome to Barcelona,' said Cruyff. 'I hope we have a good game. You notice that we have three officials. One each from Hungary, Spain and France and if you have any problems, Rodney, all you have to do is contact me because I speak seven languages fluently.'

With that we shook hands once more and wished each other luck. Christ, I thought to myself looking round at our players. Some of this lot can't even speak English properly!

Cruyff had, and probably still has, an amazing presence; and what a fantastic player he was. I suppose you could say Dennis Bergkamp is the poor man's Johan Cruyff. He played that kind of loose, forward role, dropping off into midfield, going wide, and he could be his team's 'out ball' as well when they need relief at the back. You don't really see players like that any more. That's why he stands out.

An interesting thing is that Cruyff was a heavy smoker during his playing days. Bobby Charlton smoked as well although not to the same degree as Johan who smoked at least 40 cigarettes a day before his heart bypass operation in the early 1990s. When I started quite a lot of players smoked. You would see them lighting up in the dressing-room after a game. I wonder how many players smoke today – not many I bet, thank God.

Next to Cruyff has to be Pele. Over the long haul he was the greatest player there has ever been and the difference between Pele and Besty is that the Brazilian played in four World Cup finals and was on the winning side on three occasions. Pele had a bigger stage, which is George's only regret as a player.

Edson Arantes do Nascimento was a fantastic ambassador for the game. A war was stopped in Africa for 24 hours to allow a visit from him. When I played with and against him in America, it was a boost just seeing him walk on to the pitch. We all wanted to perform like him.

I particularly like the story of an exchange between a press-man and the Brazilian coach Zagallo during the 1970 World Cup. As a player, Zagallo had been a winner in the 1958 and 1962 tournaments. The reporter told him that Brazil might be the greatest team in the world but they had a problem with the goalkeeper. Zagallo replied, 'Unfortunately, my best goalkeeper also wears the No. 10 shirt.' To me, that sums up Pele as an athlete. It's a little known fact that he had a 39-inch vertical jump, which is only marginally short of American NBA basketball players.

Pele also had the hard streak that you need to play at the top level. It's not something you can develop; you have to be born with it. When you are provoked, it has to be there. I had it. Besty had it, too. Steven Gerrard and Michael Owen have it – baby-faced they may be but they've got an edge. I wouldn't include

David Beckham in that bracket because the incidents in which he has been involved are more petulant than hard.

Alongside Pele I'd have Jimmy Greaves who was the greatest British goalscorer by a mile. Over the years, every time a young goalscorer bursts on to the scene they are compared with Jimmy. First it was Fowler, then Owen, then Phillips, and each time it is said they are the closest to Jimmy Greaves yet. That tells you something about the quality of player Jimmy was. I said it myself about Fowler at 17, but he has yet to reach Jimmy's level.

Jimmy could score goals out of nothing. His best trick was to disappear from a game, leaving you wondering if he'd ever been on the pitch in the first place, then bang. You'd be two goals down thanks to Jim's only two touches in 90 minutes. Sometimes I think the saying about being in the right place at the right time was invented for him. How he achieved his fantastic goal haul is beyond me. Some of it is vision but a lot of goals at the top level come from just one touch. You don't get the time to control the ball because your response has to be instant. Jimmy had terrific speed over short distances but the most fascinating thing about him was his composure.

Jimmy's finishing was natural and unique. I tried to copy the way he hit the ball so early but you couldn't learn it – it was instinct. The ball was often past the goalkeeper before he had even seen it. Jimmy had very little backlift, which keepers hate. They like to see you winding up so they can tell where and how the ball will be going.

Jimmy scored on his debut for every team he played for – Chelsea, AC Milan, Spurs, West Ham and England. In the season before he left for Italy, he scored 41 league goals and a record six hat-tricks. Never mind Manchester United, the Bank of England couldn't afford Greaves if he was playing today. His record stands up to anybody's in any era. Jimmy has said that his short spell in Italy was an unhappy time for him, but he still hit the target nine times in 14 games. Bobby Charlton is England's top marksman with 49 goals in 106 appearances, but Jimmy's total of 44 in 57 games between 1959–67 is just astonishing.

During the 1961–62 season he went to Spurs from AC Milan for the odd fee of £99,999, but he could have doubled his pay packet by returning to Chelsea, as he described in his book *The Sixties Revisited*:

> For me, a transfer to Spurs was like being given a passport to paradise. I was so keen to join what I considered the best team in Europe that I agreed to a wage of £65, less than the £120 a week Chelsea dangled in front of me. So much for all the bunkum about my having been a greedy money-grabber. I came home from Italy virtually penniless. Much of my £4,000 signing-on fee had been eaten up by legal fees and air fares.

How many players, let alone top internationals as Jimmy was then, would do something like that today? I'd say none.

Apart from brilliant playing skills, there are other traits that footballers must possess which are not so obvious to the fans. They are essential to the success of a team and therefore no less significant. I've chosen the substitutes to reflect those qualities.

My first guy on the bench would be the former QPR full-back Tony Hazell because I have rarely met a more genuine lad than him, and that's a quality sadly lacking in football nowadays. What Tony would bring to the dressing-room is an indefatigable spirit. Never once did I see him down during or after a game. Every winning team has to have someone with the ability to lift spirits because, believe me, there are times when footballing skills are not enough. Vinnie Jones did that job splendidly for Wimbledon and he was bought by Leeds, Chelsea and Sheffield United for what he could do for a squad. Tony is very different from Vinnie but he had, and still has, the ability to make you laugh and smile when you most need a boost.

Hazell also strongly believed in his own point of view and would argue it to the hilt against anybody, even if he was wrong. Sometimes during a discussion about football he would become so passionate that he would cry. Passion like that can often galvanise other team members. Tony had 14 fights during his time at Loftus Road and never landed a punch once. It's true that Tony was a bit short on skill, but he's a priceless character and characters like him are few and far between.

Next on the bench would be Asa Hartford because anyone who can play football at the level he did with a hole in his heart deserves to be in any all-time great side. For all that, I always thought Hartford was a terrific player. He had two tidy feet, could tackle ferociously, pass beautifully and possessed an engine that defied his handicap.

Asa could also double as the nightlife reconnaissance expert. When I was with Manchester City no one was better at finding out the best clubs and bars. You may laugh but this is an essential quality for any travelling side – a happy team is a winning team.

I would also include the late and great Bobby Keetch. Never has there been a funnier man in football, or one with such a brilliant mind. Bobby had a fantastic sense of humour. He could tell more jokes than Morecambe and Wise and a dressing-room would never be a dull place with him around. Keetchie would have you in stitches. I could be here all day telling you legendary tales about this cracking man. Here's just one I witnessed myself at Fulham towards the end of the 1964–65 season. Vic Bucking-ham, the manager, called the players together for a pep talk. We had been having our usual struggle to stay in the top flight and, with 10 games to go, we were languishing near the bottom of the table. To give everyone a lift, Tricky Vicky told us, 'We're in desperate trouble lads but if we stay up, there'll be something for everybody. I can't tell you what it will be right now although what I can say is you will definitely not be disappointed.'

I've never thought anything like that affects a result because you're going to play the best you can anyway. Nevertheless, we all rubbed our hands with delight at the prospect of a mysterious gift.

Fulham avoided the dreaded drop on the final Saturday of the season, not through our fighting spirit but because of the poor form of Wolves and Birmingham City who went down instead. After the game, Buckingham told everyone they would get their reward at Craven Cottage on the following Monday morning. When I got there, the whole first-team squad were acting like it was Christmas. Everyone was laughing and as excited as children. Buckingham appeared at the door of the changing rooms and said, 'In the referee's room at the end of the corridor are cases and there is one for everybody. In an orderly fashion, just walk down there and collect one of the boxes. But don't rush. The contents are fragile.'

We were pushing and shoving each other as we made our way to the official's room where I thought we might get a Harrods hamper or better. When we got to the referee's room, there were 25 boxes of red and green apples that Buckingham had got from a farmer he knew. That was the Fulham players' bonus for escaping relegation. Keetchie just shook his head at Buckingham.

'You're having a laugh,' he said. I'm positive he was the man who coined that phrase. I'd never heard it until I met Bobby and I'm an East London boy who grew up with all those expressions.

Every winning team has a minder, one tough guy who everyone respects. Some of the biggest players I've known have often acted like babies so it's much more than mere muscle. It's a mental attribute. For me, the hardest man on the pitch during my playing days was Tommy Smith. The hardest player off it may surprise you – Mark Lazarus, the former QPR winger who would be a certainty for a spot on my subs' bench.

Mark came from a very tough boxing family and he had no problem having a row with anyone. He didn't look for trouble but when it came his way, look out. Lazarus could stand up like one of the old-fashioned bare-knuckle fairground fighters.

One day at Rangers we were playing a five-a-side during training. Mark was on one side and Tony Hazell was on the other. Unfortunately, the game got out of hand and the tackles began flying in until Hazell produced a very late challenge from behind on Lazarus. Mark got the hump, but Bobby Keetch quickly sorted it out. Two minutes later, Tony clattered Mark in a similar fashion and the trainer called a halt.

Walking back to get changed, Mark said to Tony, 'You were out of order there and you're very lucky I didn't give you a crack.'

Amazingly, Hazell replied, 'I don't know what you're talking about, you bastard. Go and have a lie down.'

Before Tony had finished speaking, Mark, with all the technique of a professional fighter, had struck him on the side of the head cutting his eye open. We all stood there with our mouths open as Tony hit the floor, spark out with blood all over his face. Keetchy brought him round with a sponge and bucket of water, and cleaned him up. The eye needed stitches. Tony wasn't finished, though, and he walked right back to the changing room where Mark was dressing and had another go. If we hadn't dragged Hazell away, Mark would have seriously hurt him.

Now this is the point. There are people who are hard on the pitch, there are even people who are violent on the pitch. Then there are people who are just hard wherever they go. On the pitch, Mark Lazarus was a nice ball-playing winger, with no malice in him. He would understand hard tackling and every-thing that goes on in a game, but a deliberate attempt to hurt him would have been a serious mistake, as opponents would worry in case Mark decided to get his own back. With someone like Lazarus around, the team would never be intimidated.

My final substitute would be Kevin Keegan for his work ethic and sheer enthusiasm. I first met Kevin when he came into the England team for the fixture against Wales in 1972. He had the personality of a parking meter but what an exciting player, just the sort I would have in my team any day of the week.

When you pick a side, you have to think of all situations, particularly when it's a cold day and you are away from home. The players you want then are those like Roy Keane, Patrick Vieira and Kevin Keegan. I never played with Keane or Vieira, so I'll select the player from my era who epitomises not only skill but guts, determination and the will to win.

Kevin had all that and more but I don't think I've ever met anyone as quiet in the dressing-room. He must have developed his charisma later on because he had none then. I remember having breakfast with Kevin and three other England team members and he didn't say one word throughout the meal.

I hold Keegan up as a role model for any young player today. When you talk about footballers making the most of what they have, Kevin is top of the pile. He had to graft to get to the levels that he did and he went on not only to captain England but also to hit 21 goals in 63 games for his country. When he was at SV Hamburg, he was twice voted European Footballer of the Year, which was a fabulous achievement. I think, too, that if he hadn't rolled up his sleeves, he would never have risen to the heights he did.

I'll be brutally honest with myself here because I wasn't the kind of guy you would pick for a freezing day in January against, say, Rotherham. But I was a great asset to a team who had a few players like Kevin. I would have loved to have played with Roy Keane. When Manchester United agreed to pay him £52,000 a week, I said on Sky that I couldn't believe they had got him so cheap. Roy will win you things.

But being a great player, as Kevin was, and being a great manager are two vastly different things. I didn't feel Keegan had it in him to be the England manager in the first place. He didn't have the ability to deal with what I call the intangibles. Take Arsenal and Chelsea, for example. You could argue all night about which is the better team. On paper, it would probably be Arsenal; but football isn't played on paper. A lot of times the result of a game rests on something indefinable and intangible, illogical even. It's an area that all the great managers, and in particular Brian Clough, have the ability to read.

Here's an example of intangibles. David Platt was a very good club player who became a brilliant international and scaled heights that you wouldn't have thought he could reach. Platt scored 27 England goals in 62 appearances, which is quite stunning for a midfield player today. That's almost a goal every other game and nearly as good a ratio as Alan Shearer's. Glenn Hoddle and John Barnes show the opposite side of that coin. They were absolutely brilliant club players but often seemed to struggle at international level. The point is there's no real formula for working out the intangibles. It's part of what makes football so intriguing.

CHAPTER 14

plan? you must be joking!

England are their own worst enemies.

Lennart Johansson,
Swedish president of UEFA

The Football Association believes that Sven-Goran Eriksson will
be its saviour. But I think his appointment as England's head
coach means the senior members of the FA should be sacked. The
decision to look abroad for someone to take charge of our
national side is an admission in itself that the FA has failed
miserably with the management of football in this country. The
Football Association says it has

> ... put coaching at the forefront of its long-term strategic
> plan ... The FA, through its extensive training programme
> for coaches, has always had as a priority improving the
> technical quality of coaching which would, in turn, reap
> rewards on pitches up and down the country.

Plan? Was it the FA's plan all along to employ a foreign coach? If
a foreign coach wasn't part of the plan, the system that produces
coaches is obviously useless because it hasn't provided a batch of
likely candidates as it should have. The FA can't have it both
ways.

So I say the people who have 'always had as a priority improving the technical quality of coaching' at the Football Association must go. Rights have responsibilities. If you've got the right to set the policy, you must accept the responsibility for its failure.

When Kevin Keegan jacked in the England job on 7 October 2000 after a 1–0 World Cup qualifying defeat by Germany at Wembley, Adam Crozier, the FA's chief executive, said that he and his advisers had a short list of replacements. Presumably they were part of the grand scheme. Technical director Howard Wilkinson took charge for one game, then Peter Taylor was appointed in a caretaker capacity although he was still a consideration for the long term. Others on the list were said to be Arsene Wenger, Roy Hodgson, Bobby Robson and Terry Venables.

No one can dispute that they all have worthy credentials – but where does the planning come in? The year before, Taylor had been sacked as coach of the most successful England Under-21 set-up that we have had. Wenger had never worked in this country before taking over at Arsenal. Hodgson plied his trade mostly in Sweden, Switzerland and Italy before a disastrous spell at Blackburn. Robson had already left the England funny farm after the 1990 World Cup to plough a very successful furrow in Europe. Terry we have already discussed.

Is there something I've missed? I'm darned if I can see any plan. The FA must think we are all as thick as they are. There isn't a blueprint at all. It's just a shambolic shuffle from one situation to another.

It's the FA's responsibility to produce coaches. It's their job to make sure we have people capable of being in charge of the England team, and it's their fault England struggle today to be included in the top 20 football nations in the world – not the players, not the managers, not the coaches. It's a disgrace.

The FA blame everyone but themselves. When Eriksson was

given the job, Crozier implied that English people had become insular about foreign coaches. 'Whenever you change anything,' he said, 'there are always people who want things to stay as they are.' That was the biggest case of a pot calling a kettle black I've ever heard. It's the FA who need to change, not anyone else. All those people on all those committees are concerned with self-preservation and scratching each other's backs.

The Brazilians, French, Germans and Dutch have always had plans and continuity. That's precisely why they're in the forefront of most international competitions; that and another integral part of their strategy – not dumping their biggest assets. The way the FA has treated some of the greatest players in England's history has been the biggest disappointment in my life as a footballer.

When Franz Beckenbauer retired as a player, he was given a job with the German football association and he went on to become their national coach, with terrific success. Zagallo, the fantastic Brazilian, took a similar route with his national outfit and Johan Cruyff was offered the job, although he did not accept, of technical director of Holland. The French welcomed Michel Platini into their system.

But when Bobby Moore retired he was virtually told by the Football Association to fuck off. He couldn't get a job anywhere. The FA just cut him loose because they thought he was no use any more.

Bobby played 106 times for his country, captained England to a World Cup triumph and was one of the greatest defenders, if not the greatest, that we have ever had. For all that, he was just dumped by the FA when they thought he was past his sell-by date. I took personal offence at their decision not to utilise Bobby, even though it had nothing to do with me. I still can't believe it happened. I know Bobby eventually worked at Southend and Oxford but, with all due respect to both of those clubs, what a waste.

After he died, I think Bobby was patronised. His memory

was honoured with statues and stands and such, yet nobody thought of him 20-odd years ago when he retired from playing. It's not only sad, it's also the biggest indictment of all against the Football Association. Later on, Bobby Charlton and Geoff Hurst were knighted, which they deserved. Moore was treated like a pariah.

That is not the only case although Bobby Moore is by far the biggest example of such sacrilege. Gordon Banks is another example. I think he coached at Telford once.

I have always felt that if top English international footballers are not taken into the club system, the FA should find something for them. Of course, a lot of players move into club management, but my point is that it should be a priority not to let top players drift out of the game when their careers on the pitch come to an end.

That is not the only thing the FA have got completely wrong. How in the world Adam Crozier was appointed chief executive in the first place is beyond me. That job should be held by someone who has been a club chairman for 12 years or more, understands the game, domestically and internationally, and has been in charge of players and managers at the highest level. It shouldn't be given to a marketing guy who has no professional football background. If you asked a thousand professional footballers from different eras to vote for the best person to run football in this country, I guarantee you that not one of the senior FA officials would be elected. Howard Wilkinson would get a few votes, but that's all.

You've got to pay the going rate, of course, but Crozier has a six-figure salary and Eriksson's five-year deal is reportedly worth in excess of £2 million so money is obviously not the problem.

Martin Edwards would have been a good choice for the position because at the time of Crozier's appointment he had just stepped down from a similar role at Manchester United. The likes of Bobby Charlton, Geoff Hurst and Trevor Brooking could have been on the committee to choose the next England coach. Why have a former salesman involved in the process? I'm not saying you can't have guys like Crozier in the FA, but employ them to organise the finances, sales and public relations – not on the football side for Christ's sake.

If I had my way, I would split the FA into two sections. Football people would run footballing matters; bean counters and marketing guys would be in charge of non-footballing affairs. It's as easy as that.

I could not have worked for the Football Association because I have never had any respect for the organisation as it is. Until it is run by true football professionals, I never will.

The Football Association allow themselves to be used by politicians, although I'm not surprised politicians want to jump on the bandwagon. Football has changed so much in the last 25 years, dramatically so in the last 10. If you go back to when I first played in the early sixties, very few people knew who the chairmen of clubs like Liverpool or Tottenham were. You might know Fulham's Tommy Trinder because he was a comedian on the stage but that's about it. When you got off the team coach for a game there would always be loads of kids asking for players' autographs. About 20 years ago, managers began to be asked as well; five years later it was the chairmen. Nowadays you have the amazing sight of Ken Bates or Doug Ellis signing autographs while all the players troop by virtually unnoticed. Ellis has even got his own nickname, 'Deadly'.

It's not unusual to see a club's new signing being paraded not by the manager but by the chairman. You might think that's pretty harmless but, as I keep telling people, it isn't. Nobody seems to listen, though. What it does is put a finger on the ultimate self-destruct football button. Some chairmen are now as accessible to the media as players and the manager. In my day no pressman would dream of telephoning, say, Arsenal's then chairman Denis Hill-Wood, the father of current incumbent Peter. He wouldn't have taken the call anyway. But these days, chairmen such as Bates talk regularly to the press and even lunch with them. Bates is the star of his own radio show.

Years ago, I would never have dreamed something like this would happen. An hour before one of our Sky 'Soccer Saturday' programmes was due on the air, Sir Alan Sugar telephoned me in the studio.

'I want to let you know I'm resigning tomorrow,' he said, 'and I want you to present the story properly. The reason I'm resigning is I have had enough. The fans have been threatening my family. They wait outside my house, they bang on my car after games and we've had enough. I can't take any more so I'm resigning. I'm calling you because this decision has nothing to do with money. It's purely because the fans have hounded me out.'

That just goes to show you how the game has changed. I've always felt that if you are the owner of a football club, it gives you the right to say what you want. But if you take the reflected glory, you must be prepared to take the flak as well. You can't grab all the credit and the pats on the back, then moan when it goes a bit wonky. And that is what has happened in the game today. If football carries on in this way, I think it will implode. Too many knowledgeable soccer people are being forced to leave the game when their playing careers are finished. It's all right for the big businessmen to come in and tinker with their hobby then leave when things don't go the way they planned; they have somewhere else to go. But I don't like the way the game is going in terms of fan and player power when it has this kind of influence over one person's life and family.

The situation is compounded by the number of foreign coaches and players operating in the UK. If they decide to go back home, what will be left? I'm worried that unless we change some things, not enough British football people will be around to fill the vacuum.

However, as an optimist, I don't think it's all doom and

gloom; but there are tremendous obstacles to overcome. For instance, I feel that British youth is not being allowed to develop properly because of so many foreign imports. The horror story of all horror stories though would be Sky, who have been absolutely brilliant for football in this country, pulling the plug. I dread to think what would happen then. So many Premiership clubs have elevated player salaries to such a degree that they could be bankrupt if Sky decided not to continue their support.

Even so, if you had told me during my playing days that teams in the future would kick off at eight on a Monday night and 11 on a Sunday morning just to satisfy a television audience, I would have thought you were mad. Change is healthy but not just for the sake of it. There must be a positive direction.

Here's something to think about. Where will football be in five years' time? For sure there will be a reduced Premiership, probably 16 teams. I also predict seeding in the FA Cup so that the top teams won't play each other in the early rounds because it means so much money to them; and the top European club competitions could become by invitation only. Clubs will still be able to qualify in the way they do now but there could come a day when UEFA might not be able to afford the risk of the really big outfits such as Manchester United, Real Madrid and AC Milan being knocked out. You may laugh, but I think that's a real possibility.

Another thing that has changed is the importance of the FA Cup. The championship was great of course, but when I was young it was every kid's dream to score the winning goal at Wembley. The day Manchester United elected not to compete in the competition was the day the game was taken away from the people. That decision made me very sad indeed, melancholy, in fact, especially as Wembley is to be demolished.

As football has progressed, the game has lost sight of its paramount objectives. They used to be to do with sportsmanship and keeping the supporters happy. Football fans would support their local team and go to see them in any weather. Today Manchester United fans come from Surrey and Hampshire, go to two games a year and, as Roy Keane says, eat prawn sandwiches at a match. Football has been taken away from the common people, which is sad.

I don't believe that these days the majority of players play for the love of the game as we did, and I think that trend will continue. Now money is the motivation. There is nothing fundamentally wrong with that but you have to put love of the game before the financial aspects. If you asked 100 players from my era I'd bet that 99 per cent would say they played because they loved the game. Now everybody is far more mercenary, and not just the players. Terry Venables has become a kind of hired gun, a troubleshooter. When Middlesbrough, Crystal Palace and Portsmouth considered themselves in trouble, they called for Terry. Pay him the right sort of money and you've got the best football gunslinger on your side. Nothing wrong with that but Terry can't have had much passion about any of those clubs. It was purely a case of pound notes. That hasn't always been the case with great coaches and managers. If you look back over the years, can you imagine the Jock Steins, Matt Busbys, Bill Nicholsons and Bill Shanklys of the world doing things like that? Come to that, can you see Alex Ferguson managing, say, Watford?

Loyalty has gone out the window too. Players who have spent all their careers at one club, such as Tony Adams, are very rare indeed. Years ago, it was the norm. That's what testimonial games were for – to reward loyalty. I think it was right for Ryan Giggs to be awarded one, in spite of the money he is reportedly paid at Manchester United. Before Ryan signed a new contract in 2001, he could have gone to any club in the world and earned far more than United were prepared to offer him. Loyalty must be encouraged. Some clubs, such as Coventry, are like revolving doors with Moroccans, Hondurans and Peruvians coming in and going out. I feel sorry for their supporters because they haven't a clue from one month to the next what players they'll be seeing.

Whenever I talk about what is decent in football, I always seem to come back to Bobby Moore. You couldn't find a more loyal England man. In spite of the way the FA treated him after he retired, Bobby never once criticised them. If I had won 106 caps instead of nine, I'm not sure I could have acted with such good grace.

After my debut for England – as a substitute for Franny Lee against Switzerland at Wembley in November 1971 – Bobby Moore came up to me as I was leaving the dressing-room and said, 'Rodney, we're all going to a party in the East End tonight. Do you fancy it?' I did. Mooro, Mike Summerbee and I got a lift in a limo. On the way, Bobby insisted that we made an entrance. 'We can't go in there like ordinary people,' he said. So we took off our strides in the back of the car and entered the party walking like P.G. Wodehouse's Jeeves with our trousers neatly folded over one arm.

That may have been a laugh but playing for England earlier had been one of the most miserable experiences I have had in football. I was honoured to represent my country of course, but before I came on Sir Alf Ramsey said to me, 'Rodney, I want you to play like Geoff Hurst.' I don't play that way and I was confused. When I was called up again the following month for the game against Greece in Athens, I initially decided to turn the invitation down. I just didn't want to play for England. By then I was at Manchester City and I went to Malcolm Allison and told him how I felt. He asked me what I meant and I said I didn't think it was for me. So Malcolm took me to dinner at the Midland Hotel's French Room and convinced me I should go.

I can honestly say that if Malcolm had not persuaded me, I would never have pulled on another England shirt. Even then it was touch and go whether I would turn up or not. I didn't feel I was suited to play in that England set-up. Alf wanted me to be another Hurst and that wasn't me at all. I was a deep-lying Eric Cantona/Glenn Hoddle type of inside-forward – not a hard-running front man like Ramsey wanted. I was never an out-and-out striker who was prepared to run up and down the line for 90 minutes. I was also a bit of a free spirit and frequently played the game the way I saw it. I wasn't very good at being dictated to and I don't think you can play like that when you are representing your country. That's why I never really hit it off internationally and didn't play well in six of my nine games. I had a terrific match in the 1–1 draw with Yugoslavia at Wembley and wasn't bad at Ninian Park against Wales when I scored in our 3–0 win. I also had another good show against Wales at Wembley. I never played to my potential because I was always in the forward role and didn't enjoy it one little bit. At the time, England played a 4-4-2 formation with the two strikers making cross-over runs and such. Joe Royle, Mike Channon, Martin Chivers and Brian Kidd were all very good at it, but not me.

The only reason I was selected in the first place was because of the press. The media got me in. As I had been playing so well for QPR then City and scoring plenty of goals, every week the newspapers were urging Alf to give me a chance. Very rarely did Ramsey give in to anybody, yet I believe this was one of the few times that he did.

Before one game against West Germany, he asked the team who would like to take penalties. His request was met with silence. He turned to Colin Bell then Martin Chivers but neither was very happy about the possibility of a spot kick. Suddenly, Alf's eyes fell on me.

'Rodney, surely you have the confidence to put a penalty away at Wembley?' he said.

'No problem at all,' I replied.

'Great,' said Alf. 'That's settled then. If we get a penalty, Rodney's our man.' But as he walked away, I stopped him. 'What's the matter?' he said in his usual clipped tones.

'There's one little problem,' I told him. 'I'm on the subs' bench.'

My England career came to an end after a game against Wales in January 1973. Before the match, Alf gave one of his usual team-talks. He said how important it was for us to work hard and play for each other, especially as we were representing our country. Then he turned to me and said, 'You, Rodney, in particular. I've told you before that when you play for England you have to work harder. I don't care what you've done at Manchester City or QPR but that's what you have to do for me. In fact, this is the last chance I'm going to give you. In the first forty-five minutes I'll be watching and if you don't, I'm going to pull you off at half-time.'

'Christ,' I muttered. 'At Manchester City all we get is a cup of tea and an orange!'

I didn't think Alf would hear my remark but he did. It was the last time I played for England. Alf recalled that story for his biographer, although he didn't quite get the terminology right.

To me, Ramsey was a very austere and cold man although I'm the first to say he was a great manager. I have the highest regard for him. Alf would not waver from his objective. As with most successful people, he wouldn't allow himself to be distracted.

He hated Scotland with a passion and made no apologies for it. He even used to tell his players he would be embarrassed if they lost against the Jocks. Before my one game for England against Scotland at Hampden Park, where we won 1–0 thanks to an Alan Ball goal, we stayed at Troon. When we arrived at the hotel there were at least 40 photographers and pressmen waiting outside. As we approached the steps to the doors, one little Scots guy leapt out of the crowd with a notepad and pencil and said, 'Welcome to Scotland, Alf. How do you think you'll get on?'

Not many people know that Ramsey, born in Dagenham, originally spoke with a broad Cockney accent. It's also a little known fact that he had taken elocution lessons, paid for by the

FA, around the time of the 1966 World Cup. He stopped, looked at the Scots pressman quizzically and simply replied 'Fuck orrff!' in his newly acquired proper English accent. Everyone was in stitches. On another occasion, Alf may well have said 'you must be effing joking' but that was all he said this time. I know because I was standing next to him.

Even though I struggled to fit in on the pitch, I thought the world of Ramsey for what he had achieved and so did every other guy I played with. Emlyn Hughes, for instance, loved him and if Alf had told him to kick Denis Law in the head during a game I'm sure he would have done so.

Looking back to those days, I've never really understood why Alan Hudson, Peter Osgood, Tony Currie, Frank Worthington, Charlie George and Stan Bowles got fewer England caps than Carlton Palmer. Palmer is a good player, but it's an indication of how football is going in this country. If you ignore flair and pick players just because they have a good engine, you're not going to get results at international level.

Alan Hudson won just two caps. After inspiring England to a 2–0 victory over West Germany, then the world champions, and setting up Malcolm Macdonald's five-goal spree against Cyprus, he was never seen again at international level – baffling, to say the least. I always felt that if he could have got forward a bit more he would have gone down in history as one of the greatest midfield players ever. Hudson had great vision and passing ability, and could do similar things to Bobby Charlton except score. Ironically, he was once credited with a rare goal for Chelsea against Ipswich when the ball didn't even enter the net. Everyone in Stamford Bridge had seen Alan's shot miss the goal and hit the stanchion but the referee insisted the strike should count. Hudson stood there for several minutes arguing for the referee to disallow it.

Since the sacking of Ramsey in 1974, England have completely lost their way. After 1970, we didn't appear in the World

Cup finals again until 1982 and even then we were crap. In 30 years, the only time we have looked a threat was in Rome in 1990 and that was thanks to Paul Gascoigne, a flair player if ever there was one. To win World Cups and European Championships you have got to have someone who can spontaneously change a game, somebody inspirational. All the world-class teams have had players capable of doing something different. Take Zinedine Zidane, for instance, particularly when France became world champions in 1998. He would do things that would make you say, 'Christ, did you see that?' Sadly, that's something we just don't have in English football. What's more, we don't encourage it. Until we get it back, we will always be struggling to compete at the highest level.

Under the direction of Charles Hughes, FA coaching became obsessed with the 'position of maximum opportunity' (POMO) theory, that is, if you get the ball in a certain area quickly enough, the other team will make mistakes, you will get the ball and score. There's a famous story about Hughes walking into a lecture at the FA's School of Excellence at Lilleshall during the showing of a video tape of a renowned international XI. Apparently, Hughes stopped the tape and said he couldn't believe it was being shown to young players. 'This team passes the ball too much and you won't be able to score goals in today's football if you make that number of passes,' he is reported to have said. Who had the class been watching? None other than Brazil's 1970 World Cup-winning side!

It just goes to show the mentality of the people at the FA. Hughes thought, and he wasn't alone, you had more opportunity of scoring by just lumping the ball into the box. He wanted to get away from possession football. Yet that's precisely how every great team has played – Real Madrid, the great German international sides, the Brazilians, the Italians and the Dutch of the mid seventies. Even top English sides such as Tottenham and Liverpool loathed to give the ball away. Their logic, without exception, was that if you kept the ball, the other side would knacker themselves trying to get it back. It works. You don't need to be a nuclear physicist to work it out, do you?

That's why England are still in the Dark Ages. Even today, we don't generate players who play that way. It starts from defence, but Tony Adams and Sol Campbell aren't the type of players who like to knock one-twos and bring the ball forward. Rio Ferdinand is the closest we've got to a ball-playing defender. Not until we look at football in another way will we again be regarded as one of the top international teams in the world.

CHAPTER 15

if you say it, mean it

The most you can hope for in life is to avoid personal tragedy.

Terry Venables to me, 1972

Do you tell your mum and dad you love them? If you are lucky enough to have either or both of your parents, you should, every single day. When I get to know people very well, that's what I ask them because it's so very important.

The memory of the day before Dad died and the moment when he put his arms around me is as vivid now as when it happened more than 20 years ago. It will forever be etched in my mind with Technicolor clarity. Once when I was alone, I just broke down and sobbed my heart out because I never said the final word to him – made my peace. Even writing about the experience brings tears to my eyes because I couldn't tell him that I loved him. I don't think I will ever come to terms with it. I could have hugged him. I could have taken him to that day's QPR game. I could have made him happy on the last day of his life. But I chose to go to the match alone. Does it make me sad? Desperately.

From one point of view, I've often been my own worst enemy, particularly as a footballer and possibly in my personal life. If there's an easy way and a hard way to do something, it's guaranteed I'll take the tough route. Then when things are going well I have a propensity to make life go a bit wonky with my way of saying and doing things. But that's me.

The best example I can give is when I predicted on Sky 'Soccer Saturday' at the start of the 1999–2000 season that Bradford were certainties for relegation from the Premiership. I insisted the Bantams were easily the worst team the division has ever seen. Not surprisingly, my comments offended a lot of people in the city including the Bradford chairman, Geoffrey Richmond. The following week Geoffrey telephoned and invited me to visit Bradford. He told me I had made some rather sweeping statements about his team and asked if I had, in fact, ever been to Valley Parade? Yes I told Geoffrey but I would be very happy to accept his offer if he thought he could tell me where I was wrong.

So I went to Bradford and met Geoffrey at the city's local radio station, Pulse Radio. During the live phone-in programme, hundreds of irate fans called to give me some stick over what I had said about their team. I replied time and time again that all I had been doing was being honest, telling it like I thought it was. It was only my opinion. Finally, towards the end of the show, Geoffrey Richmond hit the nail on the head when he said, 'Rodney, I have no problem about what you said. But it was the way you said it. You have offended so many people with your bluntness.'

I replied, 'Unfortunately Geoffrey, that's my style. I don't tend to sugarcoat things. If something's good I say so. If it's bad, I say that too. I'm not going to change just to suit you.'

'Well, what if you're wrong?' Geoffrey said. 'On "Sky Sports" you make these statements yet what happens if we are not the worst Premiership team? Supposing we avoid relegation. What will you do then?'

I told him again that what I had said was merely my opinion.

'Even so,' I added, 'I'm prepared to stick my chin out and say that Bradford will be relegated and if that's not the case, I'll shave my head!'

And it was a close shave for Bradford, too. They stayed up only after they beat Liverpool, amazingly, 1–0 in the last game of the season. The defeat deprived the Merseysiders of a European Champions League place. Gerard Houllier's men had probably been put off by the deafening chants of 'Are you watching, Rodney Marsh?' which echoed around Valley Parade for the entire game. A lot of people told me later that I had actually helped keep Bradford in the top flight!

As the Cheyenne Indians say, 'Even the blind squirrel sometimes finds an acorn' and in spite of what I had said, I was thoroughly pleased for the Yorkshire team because there's a place in football for battlers, providing they stay within the laws of the game. Nonetheless, I knew even then that Bradford wouldn't last in the Premiership without major surgery and I was eventually proved right.

I kept my word to Geoffrey and before the start of City's first league home game of the 2000–01 season I had my head shaved on the pitch just before the kick-off. RAM Sports, a London-based sports promotions and event management company that I have a partnership in, organised a massive production in conjunction with Sky Sports and Gillette. It was an hilarious start to the campaign. I got a fantastic reception and it raised more than £20,000 for the burns unit of Bradford City Hospital, so everyone was a winner.

I do understand the impact of my words, but I have to say what I feel is right and honest. In 1975 when Peter Swales asked my opinion on Tony Book I could easily have said nice things and taken the easy route. But it's something I've never done as a player or in life generally. I can't apologise for the reactions of others if they are afraid of the truth. For all those who have been offended by my bluntness, I think there are many more who appreciate someone who is truthful. That is why 'Soccer Saturday' has become so popular. Football fans are not mugs. They know what is genuine and what isn't. If you were in a pub or club discussing a game, you wouldn't say, 'Oh, it's a windy day and that may make it difficult for the players.' Your mates would say things like, 'Bradford are going to get stuffed because they're useless.' That can be very cutting, I know, but it's what we would say in a bar. You wouldn't dream of fannying around with things like, 'Arsenal were a bit unlucky in that 0–0 draw the other night.' Of course you wouldn't. You'd say the Gunners were crap because they missed four sitters or whatever it might be.

When George Best and I first did 'Soccer Saturday' around 1993, we talked about football as if we were in the local. Until then, football previews had been a bit flowery, which was why they hadn't been as watchable as they could have been. 'Soccer Saturday' is successful because of its integrity and honesty, and because it is live and up to the minute. If something happens, we don't wait. We go straight to the story, directly to the news. That's what people want. Before Liam Gallagher and Patsy Kensit separated, she said the Oasis singer was always glued to the show on a Saturday between noon and six. Patsy added that she would not even go in the room while he was watching it. Everyone on the programme took her comments as a massive compliment.

My media career started with a successful spell with ITV during their coverage of Italia 90 and I was employed by them again for the 1994 tournament in the USA. I was based in Boston for the group games featuring England, USA, Brazil and Germany. But not for the first time in my life, my mouth got me in trouble; I was sacked for a comment I made during the live broadcast of the England v. USA game. Graham Taylor's England side were losing to the Americans 2–0. That result would have been very bad for a manager already under pressure. I was working alongside Alan Parry, a marvellous commentator, who fed me the line, 'Well, Rodney, there are ten minutes to go. If you were Graham Taylor, what would you do?'

'Take an arsenic pill.' was my reply.

In those days, comments like that were strictly taboo and although I saw out my contract with ITV, it was not renewed.

I was operating as a freelance, which gave me the flexibility to work for other media, including Capital Radio with whom I had a concurrent contract. I had three terrific seasons with them and was offered a long-term contract by owner Richard Park as a disc jockey. That would have meant I couldn't work in football, so I turned down the lucrative opportunity. But I did continue with them as a football pundit and yet again managed some interesting live *faux pas*. During Euro 96, I was working along-side Dave Clark on the Germany v. Czechoslovakia game when Dave, now a good friend and colleague at Sky Sports, made the infamous remark that sent me into uncontrollable laughter, live on air.

'Subs tonight for Germany are . . .' and he rattled them off as normal. I wasn't paying too much attention. Then he repeated: 'Two of their better players are Kuntz and Bierhoff.' He giggled and added, 'Which sounds like a good night out to me.' I did the first 15 minutes with tears streaming down my face.

After a few years' break, I began going into Sky for the occasional slot on what was then 'Sports Saturday' with Paul Dempsey and Sue Barker, in her pre-BBC years. Initially I went in on the odd occasion when I was in the country doing the roadshows with George. Then the format of the programme changed and the 'burger bar', as it was known in the early days, was introduced. The producer Andrew Hornett had come up with what seemed like a bizarre concept of the viewer watching the panel of guests watching live games. The idea had many sceptics but straightaway it became a tremendous success and was renamed 'Soccer Saturday'.

In the early days, Mark Lawrenson, Alan Brazil, Besty and I were the regular pundits, together with Phil Thompson and Clive Allen. The show's success has much to do with the chemistry between us all and this was increased further when Jeff Stelling became the regular presenter. The laughs helped, too. Alan and I never saw eye to eye on anything. He used to talk continually about his own career and I used to pick holes in it. He was never afraid to pull me up on something and neither was I with him. The banter helped to boost the show's ratings. We're actually good buddies now.

Mark Lawrenson, as I've said, was with me at the Rowdies for a season. Phil Thompson, another former Liverpool player, is a very single-minded man and extremely opinionated. That's a bit risky for Thommo because his dress sense is easily the worst in the world. It's so bad I reckon he must put his clothes on in the dark! I like Phil a lot because what you see is what you get.

Frank McLintock, the former Arsenal double skipper, has come on board since then and we've had many a go-round. Frank lives in the past and talks a lot about the sixties and seventies when he played. I'm always having to remind him that the game has moved on. He also falls asleep during games and you frequently have to elbow him in the ribs to wake him up for a comment. It's great crack, though.

Some of the things that have happened live have been hilarious. One day a reporter came on from Brighton and said the game had been stopped because the referee had found a hole in the pitch that was nine feet deep. Jeff Stelling asked him if he was sure it was that deep and the correspondent replied that the official was, in fact, measuring it.

'That's going to be a tremendous hazard for the players,' Jeff said.

'Well, that depends on the hole's measurements,' Frank chipped in. 'If it's only two inches wide and nine feet deep, it's no problem at all.' Everyone was in tears.

The show has developed into a six-hour programme covering the whole of the Football League and Scottish League and has taken over from 'Grandstand' as the one that all football fans watch on a Saturday afternoon. What has amazed me is the number of people in football who watch every minute and take note of everything we say – in particular, the club chairmen.

I didn't realise how much influence the show had until the Bradford head-shave scenario; and then Alan Sugar calling to explain his reasons for selling Spurs. He saw our show as the best way of conveying his message, which was pretty staggering. I had interviewed him live on air at the beginning of the 2000–01 season and he'd said that he bought Spurs on 'a whim' after he and his family had watched them win the 1991 FA Cup final. If he'd known what he was in for in the following 10 years, he said, he would never have done it. Interestingly, both he and Geoffrey Richmond said they watched the show every week, and I know for a fact that most of the other managers and chairmen do too.

One of the most fascinating interviews I have done was with the former Wimbledon manager, Egil Olsen. Now we all knew Egil was a bit odd when he arrived from Norway in his Wellington boots. But I thought he was great and when we met towards the end of the 1999-2000 season, he was delightful company, eccentric and complex.

We had met previously at my local tennis club and briefly chatted about psychology and philosophy and he had told me how he was a Marxist and a paid-up member of the Communist party. We arranged to meet again in front of the Sky cameras and after a set of tennis, which I won, we sat down for a chat. Egil told me he had 45 minutes. Three hours later we were still there talking. He had told me how he loved silence, hated music, found London too noisy and craved the quiet of the forest by his home in Norway. By the end of our chat he was showing me his favourite card trick, which took him 15 minutes to set up and he still got it wrong!

Egil Olsen is a football man through and through and, in his youth, was known as the Norwegian George Best. He has enormous dignity and honesty, for which I respected him, but in my opinion, he never stood a chance at Wimbledon.

On 'Soccer Saturday' we never know what game we will be watching until we arrive at the studios a couple of hours before we go on air, and occasionally one of us will have a moan because we're watching a duff game. We have our rows and disagreements but that all adds to the fun because it's genuine. We also have a weekly sweep in the studio on the Premiership games, which I win more often than not although Frank McLintock would disagree, as usual. We're still waiting for Jeff Stelling to win one week.

Everyone concerned with the programme is great, from the executive producer Ian Condron and the director Karen Wilmington down. They all work brilliantly together, and to get it right for the six-hour show week after week is a wonderful achievement.

So I'm very happy because my career is having a bit of a renaissance now, thanks to 'Soccer Saturday'. It's great because I get to do what millions of fans do at the weekend and that is watch a top Premiership match on Sky with a lot of old buddies, which I love. The only difference is I get paid for the privilege. The way I look at it, if you're a footballer who can't play any more and you're not into coaching or management, being a TV pundit is the next best thing. Sure, it's hard work and occasionally I have a stinker like anyone else, but I thoroughly enjoy it.

My partner at RAM Sports Management is Melissa Chappell who was an assistant producer with Sky Sports, where we first became friends. When she left Sky she asked me to help her set up a sports management firm and that's what we did in 1999. When I was a player I didn't want to bother with contracts, sponsorship deals, mortgages, insurance, pensions and all that stuff; all I wanted was to play football. So I thought RAM was a great idea. It manages athletes' business affairs in their entirety, allowing them to concentrate on what got them to the top in the first place. It also provides a full service as a sports marketing and event management company. I'm one of RAM's clients, of course.

They look after most of my business affairs, including my weekly *Daily Star* column, which is an achievement in itself; and the rodmarsh.com website, which is great fun. The site gives up-to-the-minute football news, match reports, interviews, opinions, unique photographs and special offers, as well as having my daily diary entry.

The only drawback is the travelling. I frequently commute between the USA and London. Add to that after-dinner speeches, personal appearances and a TV series that RAM is producing and you can see that although this may have its glamorous side, it can also be gruelling. But it is really flying at the moment. This year, in conjunction with the Footballers' Football Channel, we have started a television series in which I interview world stars like Phil Collins and Sir Elton John.

Phil rarely does interviews but he agreed to this one, which delighted me. So earlier this year I flew out to his home in Nyon, Switzerland, where the former Genesis drummer looked incredibly happy and relaxed, probably because he had just become a father again with his third wife Orianne. Phil was great company, and explained how his life now centres around his new family and that he doesn't like to travel because he misses them so much. He also told a great story about a run-in he had had with Chelsea chairman Ken Bates.

According to Phil, it all came from a simple misunderstanding. Some time ago, he had gone to a game with Bobby Moore. They had tickets for the match but didn't have passes for a certain bar. When someone invited them in, Ken blocked their entry and said they could only come in if Phil bought the club. And he wouldn't budge.

Collins was once a Spurs fan and he also watched QPR as a kid. Nowadays, he follows the Geneva side Servette. A football fan in the purest sense, he revealed that he goes to as many live fixtures as he can and really admires today's great players like Zidane, Figo and Beckham.

A few weeks later I telephoned Watford chairman Sir Elton to see if he would be available to appear as a guest on the programme too. I have never forgotten the kindness of his Los Angeles invitation during my nightmare at Manchester City. When Elton called to agree to my request, he couldn't disguise his delight over the Hornets' appointment of Gianluca Vialli as manager. Not long after, I went to see him at his superb home in Berkshire, and he and his staff made all of us, including the programme's crew, incredibly welcome. Elton and I chatted for over an hour and his enthusiasm, passion and affection for the game was overwhelming. His football knowledge is astonishing. Much more so than a lot of people think.

Elton told me that his all-time favourite Watford player is John Barnes and he reckons George Best had the greatest raw talent of any player he has ever seen. He also said that David Beckham is a thoroughly genuine guy and more level-headed than most people think.

Elton was clearly excited at the prospect of a new era at Vicarage Road with Vialli at the helm and he even wants to change the Hertfordshire club's strip from yellow and red back to blue and white. He also defended the former Chelsea manager's decision to replace coaches Luther Blissett and Kenny Jackett.

We talked about everything including Elton's loves and regrets. He is openly gay, as everybody knows, and explained the problems and consequences that can bring in football. And Elton revealed that he is not the only homosexual football club chairman. He said he knew at least another two but discretely refused to name them.

He also told me how, before the Hornets' game at Portman Road after their promotion to the First Division in the early 1980s, both John and Patrick Cobbold were extremely anxious as to how they could adequately reciprocate Watford's legendary hospitality. Apparently, for weeks they had racked their brains for an appropriate lunch for Elton. Finally, aware of his already receding hairline, they came to the conclusion that only one menu would suffice. It was :

First Course:	*Hare Soup*
Main Course:	*Queen's Pudding with Peas*
Sweet:	*Fairy Cakes!*

Actually, telling these stories makes me think how life can change. I've mentioned before how I view my new career as a bit of a renaissance, based upon the Best and Marsh Roadshow. Before that I hadn't lived in England for over 20 years, so I find it even more remarkable that I now have the opportunity to interview international icons and appear on TV every week. However, the really fascinating thing is the number of people I come across who say they wouldn't miss 'Soccer Saturday' for anything.

Looking at how football has changed never ceases to astonish me either. Don't misunderstand me, I think change can be for the good. Whether the changes that will certainly occur in the game in the next five to ten years will be progress, only time will tell. What is certain though is that the reforms witnessed by me and my generation will be inconsequential by comparison. For instance, I am sure that within the decade, or sooner, there will be a European Super League that will run concurrently with the English Premiership. I am positive clubs like Manchester United, Arsenal, Real Madrid, Barcelona and the cream of Italy will form the nucleus of a 12–16 team Euro division.

But the season won't end there. Obviously, the side that finishes top will be the champions. However, I'm prepared to bet there will be a further competition between the top four sides who will play off for a European Super Cup. This would mean an extra two games that will take the place of the final Champions League stages as it stands today. My reasoning is based on the knowledge that the early rounds of the Champions League today are a joke because they often attract such small crowds. They are really nothing more than a nuisance to Europe's big clubs. So all the domestic champions of small countries will eventually be forced into the UEFA Cup leaving only a dozen or so elite outfits to battle it out in their own super league.

Furthermore, to accommodate this European Super League, the Premiership will be cut to 16 teams which will mean a 30-game season. In my view these two divisions would dovetail brilliantly but that's not all. I also predict these 16 Premiership sides will enter the FA Cup in the fifth round and will be seeded like the top players are at the Wimbledon tennis tournament. This will avoid the best teams knocking each other out during the early rounds.

Then, there's money, which is what the modern game is all about. Three years ago I got a hell of a lot of stick when I said that top players would soon be earning £100,000 a week. Well, I was right about that. What's more, in the next decade I can easily see the very best guys being paid £20 million a year. When I think back to when I was growing up in the game, a lot of players had to get a job during the summer to make ends meet. Don't misunderstand me though: I don't begrudge what footballers are paid today. I've got a lot to thank football for, because it has given me a fabulous springboard to many exciting experiences. And the money I earned, although nowhere near as magnificent as it is now, was always a lot better than working in the docks.

At one stage, because of all the travelling and football transfers, I owned five houses around the world, 15 television sets and five cars. For all that, I've never lost sight of where I came from. About 10 years after I left the East End, Jean and I decided to have a walk down memory lane. So, after a black-tie function in London, we went to Cooke's, the pie and mash shop in Stoke Newington. I had pie and mash and Jean had stewed eels and we sat there all togged up as other customers watched in amazement. It's true, at least for me – you can take the boy out of the East End but you can't take the East End out of the boy, particularly the decent principles of old-fashioned Cockneys.

I think I have the best of both worlds. When I think of my own family, my wife Jean and children Joanna and Jonathan, I frequently recall Terry's words about avoiding personal tragedy and they make me appreciate how lucky I have been. When he gave me those pearls of wisdom many years ago, I didn't pay too much heed. Yet as I've gone through life and seen other families disintegrate, footballing families in particular, I've grown to realise their importance. A lot of people I have known in football throughout the years have divorced and in some cases their children have grown up to dislike their parents. I find that extremely sad. It would have devastated me. I love my children more than anything in the world, as every father does. Joanna has just started a new job with a sports marketing company in San Francisco, dealing with major sports franchises in the USA. Thankfully, she is very happy.

My son, Jonathan, is president of the Marsh Group Inc., which has a property development division and a promotions and public relations arm that works closely with RAM Sports. Jon, I am very pleased to say, is doing extremely well in his executive position, so I am doubly blessed.

Jean and I are so grateful that we have children we are proud of. This year we celebrated our 34th wedding anniversary; we have known each other for 36 years.

I think I've been a good father and I make no apologies for doting on my children. I always put them first. Because of my upbringing I was determined not to do anything that would make them feel they couldn't come to me. In spite of what happened to me, I would never have hit Joanna or Jonathan in anger or wanted them to be in fear of me. They may have been frightened of upsetting me but that's different. They weren't going to grow up with the violence I endured. I made absolutely sure of that from the start.

Yet I am haunted by the memory of my late father. For what I am about to say, I make no apology, and I don't want any sympathy or understanding either. Because of the trauma of my upbringing, I have faced an enormous psychological barrier throughout my life – I have found it virtually impossible to say 'I love you'. Precious few people have heard those words from my lips. I have learned they should be used only when both people are totally devoted and immersed in one another. In the purest form, they are priceless and should be treated so. Throughout my life, I learned the hard way. If you say it, mean it. Like I said – I love football.

index

239

Best, George 19, 51, 61, 62, 67,
    88, 90, 96, 98, 99, 100–1,
    102, 103–5, 106–7, 109, 112,
    118, 119, 121, 136, 149,
    151–7, 181–9, 200–1, 202,
    228, 229, 234
Birmingham City 40, 73, 206
Blackburn 142
Blackpool 47, 171
Blanchflower, Danny 45
Blissett, Luther 234
Blockley, Jeff 115
Bolton Wanderers 18
Bond, John 16
Bonds, Billy 164
Bonetti, Peter 192
Book, Tony 60, 71, 73, 74, 75, 76,
    77, 78, 80
Booth, Tommy 60, 65
Bournemouth 45
Bowles, Stan 83, 98, 222
Bowyer, Lee 157
boxing 2, 3–4, 90–1
Brabrook, Peter 16
Bradford 226–7
Bradley, Ray 47
Brazil, Alan 157, 229, 230
Breitner, Paul 113, 197
Bridges, Barry 40, 53
Bristol Rovers 100
Brooking, Trevor 214
Brown, Ally 42
Brown, Bill 17
Brown, Max 184
Buchan, Martin 107, 108
Buckingham, Vic 15, 33–4, 205
Bulpin, Des 164
Burnley 18, 77
Burns, Colin 66
Busby, Sir Matt 19, 98, 218
Byrne, Colin 185
Byrne, Johnny 169

Callaghan, Freddie 24
Campbell, Bobby 103, 104–5
Campbell, Sol 224
Cantona, Eric 74, 157, 200–1
Cantwell, Noel 16
Capabianco, Ann 129
Carlisle United 40
Carolina Lightnin' 130–3, 134–6,
    137
Chamberlain, Tosh 25, 26
Chandler, Dean 157
Channing, Justin 142
Channon, Mick 48
Channon, Mike 220
Chappell, Melissa 232
Charles, Gary 170
Charlton, Sir Bobby 61, 108, 169,
    191, 195, 198–200, 202,
    203–4, 214
Charlton, Jack 195
Charlton Athletic 27–8
Chelsea 4, 19, 55, 106, 141, 169,
    208–9, 222
Chinaglia, Giorgio 88, 89, 90, 121
Chivers, Martin 196, 220
Clark, Bobby 88
Clark, Clive 42, 43, 54
Clark, Dave 229
Clarke, Allan 33
Clay, Ernie 99, 103, 104
Clemence, Ray 98, 192
Clement, Dave 178
Clements, Dave 114
Clough, Brian 55, 61, 209
club chairmen 215–16
Cockneys 11, 53, 236
Cohen, George 25, 29, 200
Coker, Ade 88
Colchester 40
Cole, Andy 162
Collins, Phil 188, 233
Collymore, Stan 118
Condron, Ian 232